KT-494-216

Attracting
WILDLIFE
to your
GARDEN

Attracting
WILDLIFE
to your
GARDEN

JOHN A. BURTON
Photography by
DAVID TIPLING

Published by Silverdale Books
an Imprint of Bookmart Ltd in 2005

Bookmart Ltd
Blaby Road, Wigston
Leicester LE18 4SE

Registered number 2372865

2 4 6 8 10 9 7 5 3 1

Copyright © 2004 in text: John A. Burton
Copyright © 2004 in photographs: David Tipling or as credited below
Copyright © 2004 in artworks: New Holland Publishers (UK) Ltd
Copyright © 2004 New Holland Publishers (UK) Ltd

All rights reserved. No part of this publication may be reproduced, stored in
any retrieval system or transmitted, in any form or by any means, electronic,
mechanical, photocopying, recording or otherwise, without the prior written
permission of the publishers and copyright holders.

ISBN 1 84509 163 9

Publishing Manager: Jo Hemmings
Project Editor: Camilla MacWhannell
Cover Design and Design: Alan Marshall
Artwork: Wendy Brammall
Editor: Sylvia Sullivan
Production: Joan Woodroffe

Reproduction by Modern Age Repro Co., Hong Kong
Printed and bound in Malaysia by Times Offset (M) Sdn Bhd

PICTURE CREDITS

David Cottridge: p20 (b), p56, p125 (tr) • Ecoscene: (Ian Beames) p37 (t); p48 (b);
(Graham Neden) p54 (b); p58 (b); (Robert Pickett) p59 (t) • Stephen Giesen: p32 (b)
Nature Photographers: (Tony Schilling) p50 (b); p66 (tr); (Owen Newman) p68 (t);
(Paul Sterry) p69 (t), p114 (b), p147 (t); (Mark Bolton) p114 (t) • Nature Picture
Library (www.naturepl.com): (Jim Hallett) p55 (b), (Chris Gomersall) p100 (b)
Angela Prescott: front cover (br), p29 (t) • RSPB (rspb-images.com): p31 (tr), p34 (b)
RSPCA Photolibrary: (Yuri Shibnev) p81 (b) • Steven J Brookes: p155 (b)
Colin Smale: front cover (tr), p26 (t)

t= top; b= bottom; r= right

CONTENTS

THE WILDLIFE TRUSTS

The Wildlife Trusts partnership is the UK's leading voluntary organization working, since 1912, in all areas of nature conservation. We are fortunate to have the support of more than 450,000 members – people who all care about wildlife – and some well known celebrities such as David Bellamy, Bill Oddie, Chris Packham and Nick Baker.

The Wildlife Trusts protects wildlife for the future by managing in excess of 2,500 nature reserves across the UK, ranging from woodlands and peat bogs, to heathlands, coastal habitats and wildflower meadows. We also advise landowners, work to influence industry and government, and run thousands of events and projects for adults and children across the UK.

The Wildlife Trusts' Wildlife Gardening initiatives encourage people to take action for wildlife in their own back gardens. Readers may have picked up one of our wildlife gardening leaflets or may have seen The Wildlife Trusts' Garden at BBC Gardeners' World Live, at the NEC. Visitors to our award-winning show garden included celebrity gardeners from the BBC's *Ground Force*, Alan Titchmarsh and Charlie Dimmock.

This new book is not only a fantastic introduction on how best to attract wildlife to your garden but also on how to attract the slightly rare or exotic. It also covers the more controversial areas of owning cats and how to deal with herons pinching fish and frogs out of garden ponds!

As traditional wildlife habitats in the countryside come under threat, as a result of modern farming techniques, development and water abstraction, gardens are becoming increasingly important.

Gardens today are havens for many species of wildlife, providing food, shelter and breeding grounds as well as links to urban parks and other open spaces. John Burton and David Tipling have just about covered every eventuality, from creating your own wildflower meadow to attract insects and especially butterflies and birds, right through to where best to site your home-made bird boxes and feeding tables.

Many of the 47 Wildlife Trusts, which together make up The Wildlife Trusts partnership, employ staff and volunteers to advise people on how best to encourage wildlife to their back yards. London Wildlife Trust even managed to persuade the Prime Minister, Tony Blair, to make space for a child-friendly wildlife pond in the garden at Number 10 Downing Street. It is amazing what a difference a few plants, logs or a pond can make to our wildlife, benefiting species as diverse as the Song Thrush, Painted Lady Butterfly, Common Frog or Hedgehog.

Thank you for buying this book and taking the time to discover how to create your very own wildlife haven. By buying this book you have already made a contribution to supporting the UK's wildlife. Now you just need to put words into action. Good Luck!

If you would like to know more about the work of The Wildlife Trusts, please fill in the membership form on the inside back cover, call The Wildlife Trusts' UK Office (0870 0367711) or log onto www.wildlifetrusts.org.

The Wildlife Trusts is a registered charity (number 207238).

INTRODUCTION

Ever since the first gardens were created, wildlife has been an integral part of them. Initially gardens were largely utilitarian, consisting mostly of culinary and medicinal plants – in the days before modern medicines, herbal remedies were gathered wild or grown in the garden. Yet from time immemorial, plants have also been grown simply for their aesthetic value.

However, with the desired garden plants comes wildlife, in the form of weeds and pests. Both are simply wildlife in the wrong place, at the wrong time. And our attitudes change throughout history. In the not too distant past, birds would have been attracted to gardens in order to be trapped for the pot – a practice that unfortunately still persists in Malta and a few other places. Starlings were encouraged to nest in earthenware pots, from which the plump young would be extracted just before they fledged. (In the same way Dormice were fattened for the Roman cooking pot.) But from the middle of the 19th century onwards, as the bird protection movement got under way, more and more people started to encourage birds into their gardens, simply for pleasure.

By the early 1900s the first books on attracting birds to gardens were in print, and designs for making nest boxes were available. Parallel with the growing popular interest in birds there was a change in the scientific study of them. Whereas most ornithology had, to date, been practised down the sights of a gun, the advent of field studies meant that scientists started putting up nest boxes so that they could more easily ring the young birds of certain species.

While attracting birds to nest boxes and feeders had become commonplace by the 1960s, encouraging other types of wildlife was still much rarer. But by the 1970s, wildlife gardening was becoming more popular, and there was an increasing awareness of the wildlife that could be found even in urban areas. Foxes were breeding well into cities such as London, but at the same time

Right: *Many of our cities are filled with high-rise apartments, but even several storeys high it is possible to attract wildlife; Otters have been seen on rivers in the heart of towns.*

Above: *A Common Frog in early summer. After breeding, most frogs leave their ponds, but a few will usually remain there all the year round.*

Above: *The Greenfinch is one of the more colourful birds seen in most gardens, where they like to breed. The dense foliage of evergreen trees, away from predators, is a favoured site.*

other species, such as the Red Squirrel, were fast disappearing over most of lowland Britain. Attitudes were changing – animals such as bats, once treated as pests, were attracting protection and soon bat boxes were being put up for them. Even snakes and other reptiles and amphibians were no longer being persecuted on the scale of the past – however, at the same time their decline was accelerating. Pesticides, 'improvement' of grasslands and grubbing up of hedgerows played havoc with the countryside of the 1950s and 1960s, and the destruction continued as pesticides and fertilizers were used even more intensively in gardens, and

Above: *A Comma Butterfly feeding on rotting plums. Over-ripe fruit is popular with a wide range of wildlife, so don't pick all the tree's produce and leave some to fall.*

Above: *Bank Voles are common in rural and many suburban areas, particularly where there are plenty of hedges, feeding on seeds, fruits and also fungi.*

persistent pesticides were being employed for timber treatment in buildings.

By the turn of the 20th century the countryside of most of Britain and northern Europe was largely a series of monoculture fields, broken only by ever decreasing numbers of hedgerows and ever more isolated woodlands. It is safe to say that as the 21st century dawned, the average supermarket car park contained greater species diversity than most 40 ha (100 acre) fields of farmland. And, in fact, suburban gardens are among the biologically most diverse habitats of all.

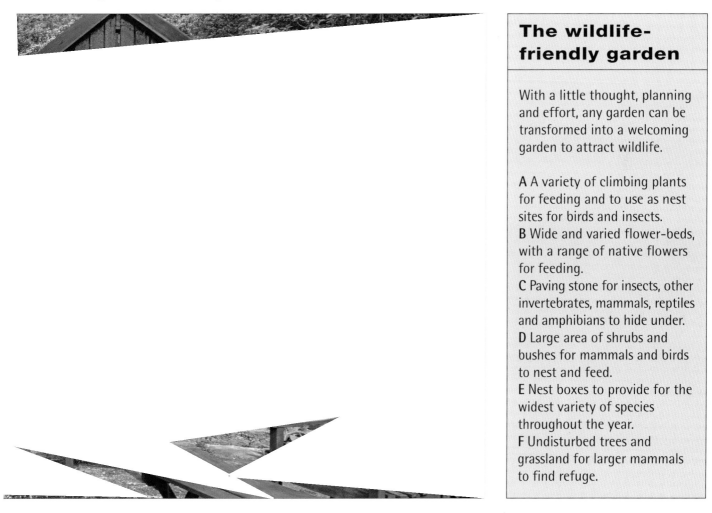

The wildlife-friendly garden

With a little thought, planning and effort, any garden can be transformed into a welcoming garden to attract wildlife.

A A variety of climbing plants for feeding and to use as nest sites for birds and insects.
B Wide and varied flower-beds, with a range of native flowers for feeding.
C Paving stone for insects, other invertebrates, mammals, reptiles and amphibians to hide under.
D Large area of shrubs and bushes for mammals and birds to nest and feed.
E Nest boxes to provide for the widest variety of species throughout the year.
F Undisturbed trees and grassland for larger mammals to find refuge.

Above: *Wild swans and other waterfowl at The Wildfowl &*
Wetlands Centre, Welney, Norfolk. The birds are fed with grain,
attracting huge numbers to this refuge, safe from hunters.

Many of the wilder and more natural areas are now protected as nature reserves, but it is worth bearing in mind that almost no part of the British Isles is truly natural – almost everywhere shows the results of human intervention. And most nature reserves need ongoing management. In this respect, they are no different from a garden. Both are habitats being managed to achieve a particular objective. Wildlife and gardening are certainly not incompatible, but inevitably some wildlife is incompatible with our other objectives – whether it be simply an attractive area to sit, or an allotment for vegetables. Left alone, certain species – usually those we define as weeds and pests, take over in the short term. Leaving everything alone probably results in lots of brambles, nettles, and possibly rats and mice. Just as on a nature reserve hedges have to be trimmed, woodland coppiced, and marshes flooded, so even in a small garden, a balance has to be maintained.

At one end of the scale, there are national parks covering hundreds of square kilometres; at the other, an urban window box. In the Pyrenees dead donkeys and cattle are put out to attract and feed vultures; at The Wildfowl & Wetlands Trust reserves bucket loads of grain are used to feed ducks, geese and wild swans. In essence this is no different from hanging peanuts out on the balcony of a seventh-floor urban flat to attract Blue Tits – just a difference of scale. But it is important to realize what is appropriate for your particular situation. There is no point in trying to attract Pine Martens, unless you live in an area where they are present. And unless you have a relatively large garden, the chances are you won't want Moles, hares or Rabbits; they will be pests. And even if you do want them, you might end up very unpopular with neighbours.

Many years ago, I moved from the city to rural East Anglia, where for the price of a London flat, I can now live in a 16th-century farmhouse with 2 ha (5 acres) of garden, including moats, ponds, woodland and meadow. It is ideal for attracting wildlife, despite being largely surrounded by the typically desolate East Anglian landscape of vast open fields. By careful management, I have been trying to create a garden that is wildlife friendly – keeping Rabbits and other potential pests confined to the 'wildlife' garden, and keeping vegetables and flowers to rabbit-free areas. By planting flowers and shrubs known to attract wildlife, and providing potential

nest sites and shelter, I may not be contributing to a great increase in numbers, but I certainly find it easier to see and watch wildlife.

How to use this book

The first section contains general advice on creating a garden that is attractive to wildlife, and is illustrated with many of the features that will make a garden suitable for a wide range of animals from birds to insects and from amphibians to shrews. It deals with nesting and roosting boxes, as well as the foods for different species, planting, and creating ponds.

The second section is a directory of garden wildlife. While it is not exhaustive – there are far too many invertebrates for that to be possible, it does describe many of the most obvious and commonly encountered species, and in particular those that most people will want to attract. Each species is described, and details of their habits, breeding and food requirements are given.

The third section gives references and information about organizations, so that you can follow up your interests in more detail. Since most information is now available on the internet, several useful websites have been included.

Above: *A pottery bell used to contain suet-based bird 'pudding' is a favourite with tits, such as the Great Tit (above) and Blue Tit (below) shown here.*

Below: *Small Tortoiseshell Butterflies. They are often abundant in late summer, after the young have fed on nettles. Like most other butterflies, the adults feed on nectar.*

PLANNING A WILDLIFE-FRIENDLY GARDEN

Before starting a wildlife garden it is well worth finding out about the wildlife of the area. You can do this by reading the reports of the local wildlife society, bird club, or county wildlife trust. Most areas of the country are covered by such organizations, and many of them now have web sites. This way, you will know what species of birds and other animals are likely to occur, and hence which sorts of feeders and nest boxes you could put up. It is always worth joining at least one of these organizations – that way you will not only be kept informed, but will also be helping to conserve wildlife.

Whether you have 10 square metres (107 square feet) of urban backyard, or a 400 ha (1000 acre) nature reserve, the basic rules for attracting wildlife are essentially the same. Most animal species require one or more of the following if they are to be persuaded to visit: food, water, nesting sites, roosting sites.

The larger the garden the more 'natural' it can be made to appear, though do be warned - creating some 'natural' habitats can involve a lot of hard work. But whatever the size of your plot, planning is essential, and

the longer the timescale you can devote to working on your garden the better the final result is likely to be. In these days of TV make overs, there is a tendency to expect a garden to be transformed over night, yet a really good garden for wildlife takes many years to mature. So if you have any big trees, treasure them whatever the species. There is a tendency among many nature conservationists to be dismissive of exotic trees, but many of these species have been with us for so long they are to all intents and purposes native, so much are

Opposite: *A large garden gives ample opportunity for creating habitat for wildlife. This flower-rich wet area will attract a wide range of insects as well as birds and other wildlife.*

Below: *A varied garden that manages to provide some interest for wildlife, but it would be even better if the grass were left to grow longer in some areas.*

Above: *A male House Sparrow. Once abundant in both town and country, its numbers have dropped catastrophically.*

Below: *A wet, marshy edge to a large pond is possibly the best habitat of all to create in a garden if there is enough space. And many of the marsh-loving plants are very attractive indeed.*

they part of our natural ecosystems. And they should be particularly welcome if they are big, providing a wealth of shelter for birds and other wildlife.

The plan

The first step in planning a wildlife-friendly garden is to draw up a rough plan. Start by drawing a scale plan, preferably on squared paper, indicating on it any significant existing features that you wish to retain. Large trees, garden ponds, sheds, lawns, children's play area and so forth. Next, using this book, decide what your objectives are. This will depend largely on where the garden is situated. If it is in the middle of a town, then it is unrealistic to expect to attract snakes, deer or Badgers. And even if you live in the country, if you have pets and small children, you probably will not wish to attract Adders. But Foxes and birds may be possible. However, do bear in mind potential problems with neighbours when planning. A neighbour with pet Rabbits or Guinea Pigs may not be too enthusiastic if you encourage Foxes to build their den under your garden shed. (I was amazed to see how a Fox had bitten through a well built run to get at, and kill, a friend's Rabbit; it was only after analysis of hair from the cage that we finally accepted it was a Fox.) It is very important during your planning to remember that rats and mice are also wildlife, and are very easily attracted,

but may not always be welcome. Also, if the garden does not have a pond, always try to include one; water is an excellent way of increasing the variety of wildlife.

The next stage is, I believe, essential; when I first tried planning a garden, the owner of one of the finest 'natural' gardens I have ever seen, advised me that the most important part of planning was to plan paths, and make them wider than you thought necessary. This has always been valued advice, and is definitely true. Whether the paths are mown grass, paving, bricks, gravel or bark, they should be generous enough for two people to walk side by side. Another piece of advice, which I confess I have rarely followed, is always to plan the planting, and plant in large groups, and not succumb to buying single specimens from garden centres and then try to find a place for them. This, of course, is easier said than done.

Finally, decide where you want to put your wildlife feeding stations, ponds, and any other garden features, such as rose arches, and other wildlife sites. Keep in mind all the time the other uses you want for the garden. An attractive children's recreation area, a patio for barbecues, places for sitting and contemplating are all compatible with wildlife; the process just requires a

Above: *Common Toads mating. The males are much smaller than the females, and wait at the water's edge for them to arrive at the pond. Toad spawn is laid in long strings.*

Below: *A good wildlife garden will contain a flower-rich meadow to attract bees, butterflies and other nectar feeders.*

bit of thought. And, contrary to what many TV gardening programmes suggest, the best gardens evolve; they do not happen overnight.

The Wildlife-unfriendly Garden

Lack of imagination and effort will result in a sterile, hostile environment, attracting few wildlife species. Straight lines dominate, creating isolated, unproductive areas. Note the lack of suitable food plants, bird tables, feeders, or places to nest and roost. Short-cropped lawns provide little cover for wildlife, about the only thing that can be said for this garden is that birds can see predators a long way off. It is, however, a garden that is easily made more wildlife friendly.

Key:

A Large, well-manicured lawn.

B Long, narrow flower-beds, planted with exotic, non-native flowering plants unsuitable for wildlife.

C Thick leylandi, suitable for roosting but little else.

D Bare garden fence, without any climbing plants.

E Large patio.

F Pond with large Koi.

G Cats allowed free access to the garden will scare many birds away.

The Wildlife-friendly Garden

With a little thought, planning and effort, any garden can be transformed into a welcoming, friendly environment to attract wildlife. Note the absence of straight lines, and the gradual shift from one area to another, creating a continuous series of mini-habitats. The key to attracting wildlife into a garden is to ensure there is water and that there are as many different habitats as possible. If feeders and artificial nesting sites are then added, the possibilities are almost limitless.

Key:

A Lawn areas allowed to grow much longer and only mown after the grasses and flowers have seeded. A bird bath and an array of bird feeders.

B Wider, more varied flower-beds, with a range of native flowers for feeding, shrubs and bushes, for nesting, roosting and feeding and climbing plants to use as nest-sites.

C Fruit trees produce food for both the gardener and wildlife.

D Log and rock pile.

E Small pond, with marshy edges, creating mini-wetland habitat.

F Compost provides nutrients for the garden and also a rich habitat for invertebrates and shelter for other wildlife.

G Mown path.

H Feeder for nocturnal mammals.

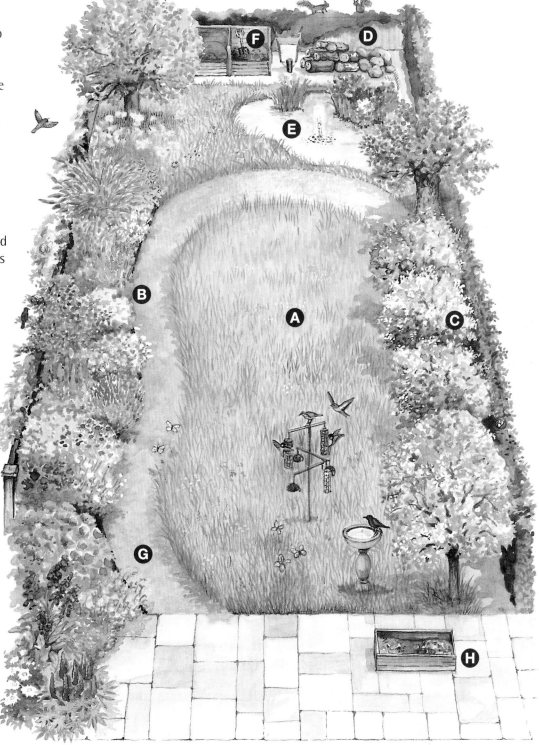

THE LAWN

Unless they are very small, most gardens still have a lawn, and the lawn is a good place to start wildlife gardening. Modern lawn mowers can be very destructive, particularly if they mow close to the ground, giving insects such as grasshoppers little chance of survival. By simply not cutting the grass too short, you will make it more attractive to a wider variety of wildlife, and by not spraying or digging out daisies and other 'weeds' the diversity will soon increase. You can, with a minimum of effort, help this diversification on its way by planting seeds or plug plants. Cowslips are particularly easy to propagate in this way. Grow from

seed a few trays full of plugs, and then plant them out, about 20 cm (8 in) apart, and within 2–3 years you will have a meadow-like lawn in spring. Once the cowslips have flowered, you can mow the lawn but set the blades high. It would be nice to add orchids, such as the Green-winged Orchid or Bee Orchid, but, although propagated specimens can be bought, they are too expensive for the average gardener. However, there are plenty of wildflowers that can be grown in plugs then planted in an existing lawn, as an effective way of transforming the lawn in a couple of seasons. I have also successfully planted seeds in the bare earth thrown up by Moles.

Above: *Cowslips are attractive, long-stemmed relatives of the primrose. They are easy to naturalize in a lawn, provided it is not cut short, and is not mown before early May.*

Below: *A wildlife-friendly lawn with daisies. A flower-rich meadow can be created if mowing is postponed until mid-summer, ideally after June.*

WATER AND PONDS

Water features became the gardening fashion of the late 1990s, but water is also invaluable for attracting wildlife. Bird baths have long been a characteristic of any garden designed to attract birds; however, running water is an even better draw. Birds, such as Redpolls, flying high overhead will notice the movement of the surface and descend to drink. Ensure that there are plenty of safe, shallow places for birds to settle around the edge of a large pond.

Ponds are probably the single best way of attracting wildlife to a garden. And don't be put off by fears about small children falling into them. There are plenty of ways of making ponds safe. If the pond is sited in the corner of a garden, it is relatively easy to fence the area off, with a pretty picket fence, or some other design appropriate to the garden, and to keep the gate padlocked. The pond should be shallow, with soft edges. In many of the cases where children have had accidents involving garden ponds, they have fallen on a hard edge of stone and been

Above: *A Starling drinking. Common enough to be disregarded, Starlings are in fact beautiful birds, with iridescent plumage.*

Below: *A healthy garden pond. It is important to keep nutrient levels low in a pond to prevent algae.*

Above: *Grass Snakes, easily identified by the yellow 'collar', are very aquatic, feeding on fish, frogs and toads, and often float on the surface sunning themselves, ready to dive to safety.*

knocked unconscious. With well-planted margins, children are also less likely to fall in. Finally, children should grow up regarding a visit to the pond as a special treat, only done under supervision when they are very young.

My view is that the larger the pond, the better – within reason and in scale with the garden. Ideally, a pond will be big enough to have shallows in which marginals can grow. Many of these marginals can be extremely attractive; sedges and grasses provide shelter and interest all the year round, and flowers such as kingcups and yellow flags add a seasonal splash of colour. In a small garden, a pre-formed glass fibre pond is the easiest to install, and a local garden centre will usually have a selection of shapes and sizes. Larger ponds will need to be lined, unless your garden is on heavy clay. Unless you are very fit and enthusiastic, don't attempt to dig it by hand – mini diggers are very cheap to hire, and will dig as fast as the soil can be barrowed away (and can be great fun to operate, if like me you spend a lot of your time at a desk).

When planning the garden, if you are to have a large pond, do plan where to put the soil, remembering to keep the topsoil to one side if you are going to need it to cover any subsoils.

Below: *Lesser celandine provides a splash of brilliant yellow colouring in spring in shady areas under hedges. Although it spreads, it is relatively easy to control with hand weeding.*

Below: *Arrowhead is an aquatic plant whose characteristic arrow-shaped leaves only show when they finally grow above the water's surface.*

Above: *Damselflies, such as these Azure Damselflies seen here egg laying, are easily attracted to quite small ponds. They are one of the most common and widespread species.*

Fish for ponds

If you want wildlife such as newts, frogs or toads to use your pond, then the best advice is: do not stock any fish. Most species of fish will eat amphibian eggs, and male frogs in the breeding season will often strangle fish such as Goldfish. Even small fish such as sticklebacks are voracious predators of amphibian eggs and larvae. If you do want fish, then the best solution is to have two ponds – perhaps a small, formal, relatively shallow pond where ornamental fish can be seen and fed (and are more easily protected from Herons), and a larger, wilder pond with marginals for wildlife. If you have really large ponds and want to stock them with native fish, you should consult the nature conservation authorities, or your local wildlife conservation trust (see page 156), for advice on the best species, and sources. But the best advice for the average-sized garden is to keep fish out of a wildlife pond.

If the pond is large enough, it is well worth creating a shallow slope on at least one side, so that in summer when the water levels drop, there is an area of exposed mud. This will almost certainly attract wagtails, and may possibly tempt the occasional sandpiper on migration, or a Snipe or Water Rail during the winter months. But it is important to prevent vegetation taking over the entire margin of the pond.

Below: *The yellow water lily thrives in ponds and slow-flowing rivers and streams. It has a characteristic fragrance smelling of alcohol. It will also help reduce the insidious growth of algae.*

PLANTING

Planting is both the easiest part of gardening and the most difficult. It is easy because in most cases, once the ground has been prepared, it is a job that takes a few minutes, and is very satisfying. It is difficult because first of all, all the other decisions need to have been made. The planting scheme must not only fit into the overall plan, it must also be suitable for the soils, climate and the size of garden. Unless the plants are annuals or biennials, it is important to know what they will look like in five or ten years' time. One of the key features that most wildlife gardeners should look for is low maintenance plants – species and varieties that are reasonably hardy, tough, pest and disease resistant, and will not require constant attention. What you grow will to a large extent depend on the size of your garden. It is all very well for me to advise that a decent-sized blackberry patch and a nettle patch are an essential part of any wildlife garden, but if you only have 30 square metres (320 square feet), you are not likely to enthuse over the prospect of your space being taken over in this way.

Above: *A female Blackbird. When sites are in short supply Blackbirds will nest in sheds and other man-made sites.*

Below: *Cotoneaster is a good example of a popular garden plant that produces a heavy crop of berries, which will provide a useful source of food for birds in winter.*

Shrubs for shelter and shrubs for food

One of the great advantages of shrubs is that they are generally low maintenance. A mixed hedge provides habitat for wildlife, and a hedge containing beech, hornbeam and oak will hold its leaves for most of the winter if clipped annually. Not only are such hedges

Below: *Haws, the berries of the may tree, better known as hawthorn, are an important winter food for birds as well as mice and voles. Flocks of thrushes often strip hedges of their berries.*

24

attractive, but they also provide shelter for birds and other wildlife and help to create a micro climate within the garden. Native evergreens such as box and yew also provide ideal hedging, and are very slow-growing, needing clipping only once a year. Their dense foliage is ideal for many hibernating insects and spiders, and small birds such as Wrens and Goldcrests hunt in them as well as using them for roosting. Berry-bearing shrubs similarly provide splashes of winter colour, as well as food for birds and small mammals.

Trees

Trees provide structure and often colour in a garden. While in most cases native trees are to be preferred, in town gardens exotic species can be appropriate. Species such as the London plane (actually a hybrid) thrive in the relatively arid habitat of a town, and also managed to survive the heavily soot-polluted atmosphere that prevailed throughout the 19th century and until the 1960s. In fact, the first London planes, planted in the 17th century, are still growing.

I personally think that more fruit trees should be grown. There are many trees bearing interesting varieties of fruit that are unavailable in supermarkets. The blossom of most fruit trees makes a stunning display in spring, and if you leave some of the fruit they produce on the tree and the windfalls on the ground, they provide a feast for Fieldfares and other thrushes in

Above: *The diminutive Harvest Mouse has a prehensile tail, which it uses as it climbs in search of food – here on a guelder rose. In addition to seeds and berries, the Harvest Mouse eats a variety of insects.*

Below: *A Tree Frog sunning itself. Although common and widespread in many parts of continental Europe, the species is absent from Britain, despite attempts at introduction.*

Above: *A Lime Hawkmoth, one of the more common and widespread hawkmoths, often encountered in suburban areas, particularly where lime trees have been planted.*

Below: *The brilliant reddish pink berries of the spindle tree; the rather insignificant greenish flowers appear in May and June.*

winter. Quinces and medlars are particularly good in this respect, as they ripen late. You can plant mistletoe in the bark of apple trees, providing more berries for birds in the depth of winter, and the bark of an ancient apple tree is often a micro habitat of its own, supporting a wide range of lichens and invertebrates. Cherry trees make a splendid show in blossom time, though I have rarely harvested a single fruit – the birds always manage to harvest the day before they ripen fully.

An important point to watch is the rootstock. Most fruit trees sold in garden centres are grown on dwarfing rootstocks. This is ideal for most suburban gardens, and means that even in a relatively small garden half a dozen trees are feasible, but if you have a larger garden and want to plant a tree that will one day be big, you will have to search a bit harder. Another type of fruit tree that has become popular in recent years is the 'family' tree, which has fruits of several varieties grafted onto a common stock. Family trees are widely available in garden centres and are ideal for small urban gardens, and can even be grown in large pots and tubs.

Trees for coppicing

Coppicing (cutting at ground level) and pollarding (cutting above browsing height) was an important part of the rural economy, and carried out for a wide variety

Below: *The vibernum or guelder rose is a typical shrub of hedgerows, with flat-headed clusters of white flowers in summer, and glossy red berries in autumn.*

of reasons – it provided browse for cattle, faggots for burning, poles and sticks for building and thatching, charcoal and many more useful products. But it is now practised on only a small scale, which is a great shame, as coppiced woodlands made interesting habitats for a large number of species. Dormice hibernate in the base of hazel coppice stools, and a rich variety of woodland-glade flowers flourish in the glades between stands of coppice. Coppicing is an ideal way of keeping plants that would otherwise be too big for a small garden at a manageable size. Species such as hazel, field maple, dogwoods, and willows all flourish as coppices, and willows and alders make particularly attractive and rapid-growing pollards. In addition to their usefulness for wildlife, they may be chosen for their beautifully coloured bark, and are available in a variety of different forms. Beech, hornbeam and oak were also traditional pollards, and when old, provide holes for bats as well as birds and insects. Hedging is actually a form of coppicing, and like other coppices, provides a valuable, dense habitat for wildlife.

Above: *Cutting and laying a hedge. This is a traditional art that has enjoyed a revival, and provides excellent habitat for a wide range of wildlife species. It was originally intended to provide a stock-proof barrier.*

Below: *Bullace fruits, a close relative of plums, are found in many older hedges. The fruits are often rather sour, but in addition to providing food for many birds, make excellent jam.*

Below: *The sweet chestnut is a native of southern Europe, but widely introduced further north. The nuts are a favourite food of squirrels and other wildlife.*

Above: *Blackberries are the fruits of a complex group of closely related species. They are a favourite food of humans as well as wildlife. A bramble patch also provides safe nest sites for birds.*

Below: *A female House Sparrow feasting on blackberries. A bramble patch provides a feeding place for a wide variety of wildlife, safe from cats among the prickles.*

Wild patches

If you have the space, then wild patches are certainly desirable and, unless you have a very tiny garden, room should always be found for a wild patch – even a 2-metre (6-feet) square is better than nothing. A nettle patch is definitely a must for breeding butterflies – and is the preferred food plant for Peacock and Red Admiral caterpillars. Blackberries can be difficult to control, and so in a smaller garden you could consider planting a patch of one or more of the cultivated varieties, which are less likely to run amok. Either way, wild or cultivated, the fruits can be shared with wildlife, and it is amazing how many species will feast on ripe blackberries - warblers and thrushes, as well as mice and voles. Perhaps more surprisingly, Common Lizards and Foxes are also among the species that will be attracted to blackberries and other soft fruits. In fact, if you want to grow any soft fruits, such as loganberries, raspberries and gooseberries, in your garden and eat them, you will certainly need to protect them from the depredations of birds. I once had a highly productive grape vine, but as soon as the Blackbirds had discovered the grapes (they seemed to need to rediscover it almost every year), they could strip the ripe fruits in a few hours. One evening, I heard a tapping against a window where the vine hung down and looked out to see two Brown Rats had climbed up the vine and were dining on the grapes.

The wild patch generally ends up being around the compost heap in a small garden, and it is here that a Hedgehog is likely to make a nest in which to breed or hibernate, so always be careful when tidying such an area. Another good place to leave as wild as possible, in a larger garden, is a hedge bottom. Don't tidy it too much, let plants grow beneath the shrubs and trees of the hedge – in rural areas this is one of the places where Harvest Mice are most likely to be found.

Food plants

If you want butterflies and moths in the garden, it is important to ensure a supply of the right food plants. These are too diverse to list, but a good field guide to the caterpillars of butterflies and moths will assist you (*see* page 158). Fortunately, some weeds, such as ragwort and nettles, are food plants for attractive butterflies and moths, and these plants are all too easy to grow.

Scented and nectar plants
It is essential to plant a range of scented and nectar-bearing plants if you want to attract butterflies and moths. Honeysuckle is one of the best. Not only is it a

native species, but it has also been bred in many extremely attractive varieties for the garden. For butterflies, day-flowering plants, such as buddleia, are important, but for hawkmoths and other nocturnal insects it is important to have night-scented flowers such as tobacco and evening primrose.

Right: *Cinnabar Moth caterpillars are conspicuous, advertising the fact that they are highly poisonous to almost all would-be predators. They are mostly found on ragwort.*

Below: *The Peacock Butterfly is one of many species attracted to buddleia or the butterfly bush. It hibernates and is often seen flying in early spring.*

Above: *Hedgehogs often use compost heaps and leaf piles to make their nests – so always use a fork with care to avoid injuring them. Or, better still, provide them with a nest box to use (see page 35). Unfortunately, many Hedgehogs are victims of bonfires during the winter months.*

FEEDING

Feeding is one of the easiest ways of attracting wildlife to a garden. In fact, with feeders, you may even be able to attract birds and insects to a window box on a balcony high up on a block of high-rise flats in a town or city. If a garden is well planted with a mixture of trees and bushes, there is a good chance that the seeds and berries they produce and the invertebrates they support will attract other wildlife, but it is possible to 'super saturate', particularly the birds, by using feeders. While it is possible to make a wide range of feeders very cheaply, and several books containing instructions are listed on page 156, there is now a huge variety of commercially made feeders, which are often designed for specific birds, and are generally easy to keep clean.

Where to site the feeders?

Since one of the main objectives of having feeders is so that you can watch the birds and other wildlife attracted to them, they need to be fairly close to a window. They should also be out in the open, so that birds feeding can get a clear view of the approach of any predator. Many birdwatchers have been dismayed to find that the Blue Tits attracted to feed on the peanuts, become the next link in the food chain of a Sparrowhawk. Usually this is because the feeders are positioned so that the Sparrowhawk can spring a surprise attack from behind bushes.

Above: *A Great Spotted Woodpecker at a feeder. Although it is generally popular, it can be a serious predator of small birds, attacking nest boxes to get at the nestlings.*

Feeder Hygiene

It is important to remember to clean your feeders regularly and wash them with disinfectant. There are many diseases that can be transmitted among birds and, with the concentrations that can occur on feeders, an epidemic could soon start. Try to clean all feeders every few weeks at least. Another point to be aware of is that avian TB can be transmitted to humans, through close contact with birds rather than by cleaning the feeders; the symptoms are flu-like, and the disease can be fatal. As well as cleaning feeders always ensure the food is not contaminated with pesticides.

Above: *An array of top quality feeders from Jacobi & Jayne outside the author's window, with Long-tailed Tits feeding. In the previous hour a dozen species were recorded.*

Above: *A squirrel-proof feeder, but not, apparently, Sparrowhawk proof. It is important to site feeders where they cannot be easily attacked by predators.*

Just as garden design is a matter of personal taste, so is the design of a bird feeding station. Feeding stations can be placed around the garden separately, or gathered together in one magnificent 'tree'. They can be made of wood and wire, or plastic, but the greater the number the better, as many birds are aggressive and will keep competitors away. Some species, such as Chaffinches, prefer feeding on the ground, but remember, surplus food may attract rats.

When choosing a site for your feeders, bear in mind that if a bird can see through a window to another window, such as often occurs when windows are at right angles to each other on adjacent walls, there may be a risk of the birds trying to fly through, and killing themselves against the glass. This risk can be reduced by placing stickers of hawks on it, or by having net curtains behind the window.

Below: *Silhouettes being placed on windows. These are particularly important when birds can see right through a room, and may kill themselves attempting to fly through.*

Foods

There are usually two factors to consider when feeding birds and other wildlife – we want to see them and we want to provide high-energy nutrition. That is why basket feeders are a good proposition – the birds have to stay around and work to get at the food. If you simply scatter nuts and seeds on the lawn, the birds will swoop down, grab a nut and then fly off into a tree to eat at their leisure.

Pet shops and supermarkets all offer a wide variety of seeds and other foods suitable for wild birds. But many nature reserves of The Wildlife Trusts and other conservation bodies also stock them in their shops – and the profits go to help wildlife. You can also obtain excellent supplies by mail order. The catalogues produced by the major suppliers of wild bird foods are generally very informative (*see* page 157).

Peanuts
Top of the list and popular with many different birds,

peanuts are an excellent source of nutrition for tits and other birds. Hang them in the red plastic bags they are often sold in and you may attract Siskins (as well as other birds). At one time it was widely rumoured that Siskins ate peanuts only from red plastic bags. Tits, woodpeckers and Greenfinches are all particularly

Below: *A Badger visiting a feeding tray on a patio. Badgers will feed on a wide range of household scraps, but are fond of peanuts as well as eggs and mince. They also like clean water.*

Above: *A feeder placed close to a shed wall covered with vegetation is an ideal place to attract small rodents, such as this Wood Mouse feeding on peanuts.*

enthusiastic about peanuts – and so are squirrels. You can also string peanuts up in their shell, as birds such as tits will spend time extracting them. Peanut granules are popular with Hedgehogs and mice and small birds. They are claimed to be more nutritious than the rest of the peanut as they are the germinating tip of the peanut, removed during processing nuts destined for human consumption as they are rather bitter. It's also a good use of a waste product.

Sunflower seed

Although sunflower seeds are cheap to buy, it is worth growing the plants in the garden as well – the flowers are stunning, and the seedheads provide a bonus supply of bird feed. However, don't be disappointed when the seeds disappear incredibly fast once the tits discover them. There are two types of sunflower seed; the black sunflower seed is the most nutritious. Shelled sunflower seed is more expensive, but probably better value, and wildlife that cannot deal with the shell (including Hedgehogs) appreciate it.

Millet

This can be bought as loose seed or as sprays on a stem as it grows. I have put out the latter on many occasions and have always been disappointed at the lack of interest shown. Most of the birds simply ignored it. But in a seed mixture it seems popular enough.

Corn (Maize)

If you have larger birds, such as ducks, pigeons and pheasants, then it makes sense to buy this – by the 25 kg (55 lb) sack; the 'kibbled' maize is the best.

Wheat (Corn)

Very cheap if you live in rural areas, particularly if you keep chickens as well, and buy it by the sack. I recently saw every species of British pigeon feeding on a patch of wheat spilled on the road – Turtle Dove, Collared Dove, Stock Dove, Wood Pigeon and Feral Pigeon. Ducks and geese are also avid feeders on wheat and other cereals. Greenfinches, Chaffinches and most other finches are easily attracted too.

Thistle

Relatively expensive and nutritious seed that is very popular with some birds, particularly Goldfinches. The seed marketed under the name thistle is usually a relative of the sunflower, also known as Niger or Nyger Seed.

Above: *Greenfinches are one of the most common visitors to bird tables, particularly in winter, when they often visit in small flocks. They are often aggressive, driving other birds away.*

Other seed

Almost any seed, such as barley, oats, dried peas, and lentils, are all worth putting out for the birds. When you check your stock cupboard and realize that some of your dry foodstuffs are a bit past their best, they will still make a welcome addition to the bird table. It is worth putting them through a coffee-mill or similar grinder.

Mixed wild bird seed

A good bet, sold in most pet stores, and available at many nature reserves or by mail order.

Below: *Goldfinches prefer smaller seeds such as thistle and other 'weeds'. Both sexes have the bright-coloured plumage, while the young have a greyish head.*

Breeding live foods

If you are serious about feeding live foods then you can easily breed mealworms. A glass or plastic fish tank, with a close-fitting, but ventilated, lid is all you need. Fill it with loosely crumpled newspaper, and sprinkle bran among the crumpled sheets (or buy a special mealworm mix), add a few mealworms, and place in the airing cupboard. The mealworms will pupate into adult, black beetles, which will lay eggs, and from then on you can have a constant supply of mealworms of varying sizes. If you have a large garden you can always adopt the method gamekeepers use to provide live food for Pheasants, by hanging up a road casualty so that blowflies breed in it, and the maggots drop to the ground when it is time to pupate.

Remember, the shortage of insects in the modern world is largely responsible for the decline of a huge number of bird and bat species, and other wildlife. Anything that increases insect numbers is likely to benefit wildlife.

Above: *A Willow Tit – which is very difficult to distinguish from the much commoner Marsh Tit - occasionally visits to feed on fat balls and peanuts.*

Fat
Suet, particularly when used to bind together seeds and raisins, makes an excellent food for birds, and is sold commercially as feed balls in plastic nets that are easy to hang. You can also make your own bird 'cakes' very cheaply – most kids love mixing them. Many different specially formulated bird 'cakes' are available from the major bird feed suppliers (*see* page 157).

Dried fruit
Raisins, sultanas, prunes and other dried fruits, either whole or shredded, are eaten by a wide range of wildlife. Badgers, squirrels, mice and voles, as well as Hedgehogs all eat fruits, and many birds, such as Pheasants, also will be attracted.

Foods for insectivorous birds, shrews and Hedgehogs
Pet shops usually stock mealworms, and fishing tackle shops have blowfly maggots, which are sold under the more attractive appellation of 'gentles'. Keeping them cool will slow down their development – but not every one likes such things in their refrigerator. Pet shops also sell food for 'softbilled birds' – the term used for insectivores by cage-bird keepers. This food will be taken by Robins, Dunnocks, thrushes and many others, though they may take a while to discover it. Some of the birdfood suppliers also stock live foods, including waxworms, mealworms and earthworms.

Below: *A Song Thrush pulling a worm from a lawn. When grass is not cropped close, it retains more moisture and a greater variety of invertebrates for wildlife to feed on.*

NEST AND ROOSTING SITES

Bat boxes

The very first bat box I ever put up was occupied by bats within a few weeks. This was real beginner's luck, because I have never ever attracted a bat to a box in a garden since. Many of the bat boxes sold commercially are not made to a satisfactory standard to be suitable for bats. And there are usually plenty of nice draught-free, secure roosting sites available, competing with the bat box. For a bat box to be used, it has to be very well made and generally must be sited in a place where there are few alternative roosting sites, such as a coppiced woodland, or a young plantation lacking natural tree holes. Suburban gardens have lots of suitable sites for bats to roost in, and the limiting factor in these areas is probably food supply and pesticides – timber treatment in roof spaces is known to have killed many bats. So if you are still adamant that you want to erect bat boxes you should buy well built boxes, preferably made from woodcrete, which is a mixture of concrete and sawdust. You should site them in groups, and you should get a copy of the

Above: *A Hedgehog nest box placed next to a compost heap, which is a favourite foraging spot for Hedgehogs, and a place in which they often build their nests too.*

leaflet produced by the Bat Conservation Trust (see page 156), for a more comprehensive description of positioning requirements.

Below: *Bat boxes are best placed in twos and threes around a tree, so that the bats can choose the box that has the temperature range that suits them best.*

Below: *The 'woodcrete' bat boxes are among the best as they provide the greatest insulation. Although more expensive than wooden boxes, they are also more durable.*

Shrew and mouse boxes

Mice, Bank Voles and shrews all climb extensively, and are quite likely to take up residence in bird boxes, particularly when they are not in use by birds. It is worth checking nest boxes occasionally during the winter months, and you may well find them full of the remains of seeds and berries taken there by mice or voles. Some bat species will also use bird boxes to roost or hibernate in. One of the important factors is probably the construction of the box. Boxes made of thin wood are quite likely to get very hot if in direct sunlight, and consequently any baby birds within will die; similarly,

mammals are most likely to take up residence in thick-walled, well insulated nest boxes, where they can be snug and warm in inclement weather. Bird boxes designed for tits, placed close to the ground, in a hedge or in thick vegetation will almost certainly become occupied by mice or shrews.

Bird boxes

Bird boxes can certainly help to increase the numbers of certain species of birds in a garden. For almost all of the species breeding in most gardens there is a wide range of designs available commercially. There are also a lot of boxes sold in pet shops, and other high street stores; some of these boxes, trays and other artificial sites may be suitable for aviary birds, but most are highly unsuitable for wild birds. You can build your own nest boxes, often for a fraction of the cost of commercially produced boxes, if you have the time and facilities. For the DIY enthusiast, some books that have working plans are listed on page 156 and there are a number of internet sites with details. It is always wise to make sure the design has been approved by either the BTO, The Wildlife Trusts or RSPB (see page 156); such boxes will be suitable for wild birds.

Structures for large birds

White Storks were traditionally encouraged to nest on houses, pylons and other structures, by placing old cartwheels there to provide a base on which to build. Ospreys have also been attracted in this way, but they can hardly be considered a garden bird. In North America, large numbers of Ospreys have been attracted to nest in areas otherwise devoid of nest sites, and some of these sites have subsequently been taken over by Bald Eagles. Perhaps one day White-tailed Eagles (the European equivalent) might nest on artificial platforms in gardens near wetlands.

Above: *There is no difference between a mammal nest box and a bird box – it is simply a matter of location. A box placed on the ground, under a shrub, is likely to attract mice, voles or shrews.*

Left: *If a nest box is placed in the open, make sure that for most of the day it is shaded by trees or buildings, so that the brooding parents or young are not at risk of becoming overheated.*

Kestrels like an open-fronted box, preferably high up. They are one of relatively few birds you might be able to attract to nest on the balcony of a block of high-rise flats. Now that Peregrines are spreading back into many of the areas from which they were once extinct and often nesting right in the centre of towns and cities, they too might use nest platforms that imitate the cliff-like ledges they prefer.

Owl boxes

Owls are relatively easy to attract into nest boxes, particularly if the boxes are sited carefully.

Barn Owls normally occur only in fairly rural areas, and if you have the space you could build a nest site out of straw bales. Nest boxes can also be placed high up in Dutch barns, in trees, and against buildings. They tend to like the site to be dark, but will also nest in quite open locations, provided the actual nest is dark.

Tawny Owls are much more nocturnal than Barn Owls, and normally nest only in mature woodland or larger trees in parks and squares in towns. Large boxes attached to the underside of branches are generally reckoned to be the most successful.

Little Owls like a nest box rather like a giant tit box – around 75 cm x 20 cm x 20 cm (30 in x 8 in x 8 in) with a hole approximately 7 cm (3 in) in diameter. Boxes sold for parrots will also attract Little Owls.

Jackdaws are also hole-nesters, and need a box of around 75 cm x 20 cm x 20 cm (30 in x 8 in x 8 in) with an entrance diameter of 10 cm (4 in).

Boxes for smaller hole-nesting birds

Boxes with holes

A wide range of small birds use nest boxes with holes. The most common in gardens are tits, particularly Blue and Great Tits, but Pied Flycatchers, Robins, and Wrens all use boxes with

holes, and an ideal hole size is about 2.7 cm (1.1 in). In many areas Great Spotted Woodpeckers prey on hole-nesting birds, and to protect against this it is either necessary to use concrete nest boxes, or have a metal shield around the entrance holes. There is a very wide

Above: White Storks, once a common sight in villages and even towns in northern Europe, are now rare. Here a White Stork is nesting on an old cartwheel.

Below: A large box placed in a wooded part of the author's garden. It is suitable for Stock Doves, Little Owls and Jackdaws – as yet it is unoccupied, possibly because it is sited too low.

range of commercially available nest boxes, and even if you are making your own, it is worth looking at catalogues, or seeing as many designs as possible on the internet.

Open-fronted boxes

Robins, Redstarts, wagtails and Spotted Flycatchers are among the birds that prefer open-fronted boxes. Some manufacturers produce dual purpose boxes that can either be open, or have a hole.

Boxes for crevice-nesting birds

Treecreepers in particular like this type of box, which, although not so common in commercial catalogues, is relatively easy to make.

Above: *A Blue Tit at its concrete nest box. This design has an interchangeable front, which allows an open front to be used, and makes it easy to clean at the end of the breeding season.*

Below: *A nest box suitable for Robins being placed on the side of a shed – a favourite nesting site for Robins. It is important to ensure that nest boxes are not sited where cats can attack them.*

Martin nests

Several companies now manufacture martin nests which can be fixed under the eaves of dwellings. These assist in attracting House Martins to new sites, and are an advantage when the martins have difficulty finding mud.

Drainpipes

Hole-nesting birds such as Sand Martins, Kingfishers and

Above: *Concrete nests for House Martins are particularly useful in areas where mud is in short supply.*

Above: *The author putting in place a Swallow nest box over the door of a wood shed. Swallows typically like dark corners, but it is important to ensure that cats cannot catch them as they enter and leave.*

Tree Sparrows will often adapt to drainpipes. Ideally these should be somewhere safe from predators, and since a high cliff is rarely found in a garden, a low bank at the edge of a pond is often the next best thing. It is easier to put these in at the time you build the pond, but they can always be added later. The birds you might attract will depend largely on location and what occurs in the area, so if you are in the middle of a town, don't expect too much, but even in a town it is possible to attract Sand Martins and Pied Wagtails. If you are building a garden wall, don't forget to build some nest sites.

Insect boxes

Many of the companies marketing bird boxes and bird feeders have diversified and are now selling an increasingly wide range of roosting sites for insects. Houses for earwigs, wintering butterflies and bumble bees are just a few. Most are also relatively easy to make. In general, a good supply of brush piles, log piles and similar habitats provide many of the best habitats for insects.

Below: *Insect tubes wedged among plants in pots. By providing hiding places for a wide range of insects, you are more likely to create a naturally balanced garden with fewer pests.*

Below: *Earwig 'roosts' placed on the top of canes. These provide well-insulated homes for earwigs and other insects. They also serve as eye protectors for gardeners.*

Above: *The wood from coppiced hazel has been stacked up to provide a brush pile that will become habitat for a wealth of insects, and also provide shelter for Wrens and small mammals.*

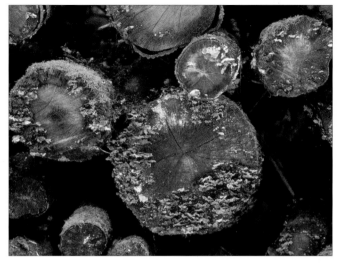

Above: *Log piles are gradually taken over by wood-boring beetles and fungi, both of which provide food for other wildlife. Fungus gnats are important food for small birds during winter.*

SHELTER

Brush piles

Brush piles are the classic shelter, important for a wide range of wildlife. Piles of twigs from tree pruning, with or without leaves attached, added to each year, provide an important shelter for small birds such as Dunnocks and Wrens. They also harbour spiders, insects and other invertebrates, providing food for warblers. If Common Lizards are present, site the brush pile so that it gets the early morning sun – they love basking in brush piles as it gives them the security of somewhere to dive away and hide.

Wood piles

Wood piles are another important habitat – so if you are felling an unwanted leylandi, use the branches for brush piles, and the trunk to form a log pile. Any untreated timber can be used to form a wood pile, but hardwood logs with the bark left on are the best. They will soon be colonized by algae and mosses, then fungi, and within the pile a damp micro climate will develop. Wood-boring insects will gradually invade, providing grubs and beetles for other wildlife to feed on. If for any reason you need to move the wood, try to reassemble it in the same structure. There is no reason why a log pile should not form an attractive part of garden design – particularly if combined with a fernery, or by the edge of a pond. In the latter situation it can be a vital part of the habitat essential to amphibians.

Left: *The Pygmy White-toothed Shrew is widespread in Europe and other parts of the world and is often found close to human habitations. It is tiny, with a body length of under 5 cm.*

Logs, boards and stone slabs

Large logs provide excellent shelter, as do sheets of old plywood and old corrugated iron. Unfortunately, the last are rather unsightly, but they are one of the best bits of old rubbish for attracting a wide range of small animals. Most reptiles and amphibians will use them, and so will small mammals. The species found will depend on the micro climate. Under a thick plank, log, stone or concrete slab, in a damp corner, newts are likely to take up residence, as well as toads and the occasional frog, particularly if it is sited close to a pond.

A sheet of corrugated iron, if you paint part of it matt black, will be used by snakes and lizards if they are present. The black-painted part will absorb heat, enabling the reptiles to warm up quickly; they will often then emerge to bask on top. Slow Worms, Grass Snakes, lizards and Adders will all use these sites – as well as mice, voles and shrews.

Above: *Adders are distinctively marked, and although venomous, very rarely cause human fatalities.*

Below: *The author with one of the sheets of corrugated iron in his garden. In a three-year period mice, Brown Rat, shrews, voles, Grass Snake and Stoat were recorded beneath them.*

41

Precautions

The golden rule is – when you have finished looking beneath them – always to replace any stones or sheeting exactly as they were and to lower them gently so as not to crush any wildlife. If there are children around, make sure they know not to jump on these wildlife shelters. Instead, give each shelter a number and get the children to do a twice-daily round, being very silent and gentle and to record what they find. It is now possible to buy concrete paving slabs specially designed to provide shelter for wildlife underneath.

Other shelter

This really depends on the size and style of garden. Old brick piles can be unsightly, but, close to a pond, newts love them. I am forever accumulating collections of old bricks, roofing tiles and similar 'spares' for the future – and as long as they are dismantled carefully, while they are awaiting use, they provide a safe haven for wildlife.

Above: *A garden shed, with a Wren's nest in a cavity in the brickwork.* **Below:** *Fledgling Robins taking their first flight from a nest in a wall.*

Sheds and outhouses

Outbuildings are often good nesting places for Wrens, Robins and other birds, as well as mice. Dilapidated sheds, old outside WCs and barns can also provide a wealth of sites for wildlife from Swallows to Barn Owls and from bats to flycatchers. In autumn several species of butterfly will seek them out to hibernate in their cracks and crevices.

Opposite: *A Barn Owl peering from its nest site. The disappearance of barns from much of the countryside has been alleviated by the provision of nest boxes.*

2

NATURAL HABITATS

The Victorians had a craze for creating 'natural' gardens, but their idea of a natural garden was somewhat different from ours. Grottoes, made of concrete-covered wiremesh, provided a habitat for dramatic ferneries, complete with trickling water, and huge blocks of slag, concrete and genuine natural rock were all used to make alpine rockeries. In the creation of these natural gardens, many areas of the countryside were quite denuded of the more sought after plants, and some areas have probably never recovered from the destructive effects of the fern craze.

Until recently, the hundreds of thousands of bulbs used for 'naturalizing' species such as cyclamen, snowdrops, narcissi, fritillaries, crocuses, tulips and other bulbs and corms were all pillaged from the wild. The destruction was so extensive that many species eventually required protection under the Convention on International Trade in Wild Fauna & Flora (CITES). This controls trade in a wide range of wildlife. The most endangered are banned from commercial trade, unless captive bred or propagated, while a large number of other potentially threatened species or look-alikes are controlled under a licensing system.

Opposite: *The South Downs in Sussex, England were once vast grassy pastures grazed by sheep and filled with wildflowers. Now only scattered remnants remain.*

Above: *Many species of bulbous plants, such as the crocus and snowdrop seen here, can be 'naturalized' in a lawn or another part of the garden – but check their origin.*

Buying wildflower seed

Now you can buy seed for a wide range of wildflowers, although it is important to make sure the source of seeds is as local as possible.

In the UK the easiest way of doing this is to visit the Postcode Plants Database on the internet at http://www.nhm.ac.uk/science/projects/fff/

By typing in your postcode you can download a list of plants known to occur in your immediate area, and the site also lists suppliers of plants and seeds.

Wildflower meadows

The easiest 'wildflower garden' to create is one of arable weeds. It is also colourful. Daisies, poppies, corn marigolds, corncockles and cornflowers were all common weeds until the 1960s, and then suddenly, with much cleaner arable crop seeds, plus the advent of highly effective herbicides, they disappeared from most of the countryside. Of course it is arguable about the 'wild' status of such flowers, since many of them are non-native exotics, which came to Britain with the crops introduced by humans. But then so are many other common plants now regarded as native. Once colourful meadows, leas and commons are now generally a uniform green, with flower-rich meadows now one of the most endangered habitats in Britain and most other parts of Europe. By mixing arable weeds with Wheat, Barley and Oats an attractive and colourful border can be created in the garden, which will also provide seeds for wildlife.

Below: Poppies were once found in almost every arable field throughout the countryside, but are now often confined to field edges and roadside verges. They thrive in disturbed ground.

A true wildflower meadow is more difficult to create, and probably needs an area of at least 0.125 ha (0.25 acres). It will also take several years to become stable, although a reasonable impression of one can be

Above: Corn Chamomile is one of several closely related species. It prefers lime-rich soils, and is a characteristic arable weed. It can be used to make chamomile tea.

Above: *Sowing wildflower seeds into roughly prepared soil. The seeds are mixed with sand to help disperse them, and also to show where they have been sown.*

Above: *The seeds have been raked into the soil, and are now being rolled. They will then need to be covered with netting to protect them from birds.*

created within two years. The main difficulty in creating a wildflower meadow in most gardens is that the soils are generally far too fertile. Experiments on nature reserves have shown that removing the topsoil is an effective way of decreasing the fertility. Failing that, it is necessary to keep mowing and removing the hay year after year. Another way would be to grow nutrient-hungry crops of vegetables such as potatoes, sweetcorn, or tomatoes, which are known for their ability to reduce nutrients in the soil. This has the added benefit of producing some food, notably organic. Planting should always be done with a mixture that is both appropriate to the soil and location.

One of the features of a good wildflower meadow is that it creates its own micro climate. The first time I made one, it always amazed me how when the lawns in other parts of the garden were dry and parched, the meadow was still lush and damp. When I came

to cut it in late June, after the flowers had finished blooming, the base of the plants would always be wet – no wonder the frogs and toads found it so attractive, and no wonder there were so many invertebrates for the shrews to feed on.

Below: *A vegetable garden is perfectly compatible with wildlife, provided you can tolerate some losses.*

Alpine rockeries

Largely out of favour with wildlife conservation-orientated gardeners, alpine rockeries were once an essential part of the suburban garden. The main problem, is that the traditional alpine garden requires quantities of stone, and in particular limestone, and that has resulted in the destruction of some magnificent natural limestone pavements. However, old brick walls can provide a similar habitat, rich in limestone mortar, dry with crevices. Chip out mortar, and grow alpines such as saxifrages as well as wallflowers (surprisingly!), and snapdragons. Leaving loose heaps of bricks will provide habitat for amphibians such as newts, frogs and toads, as well as sunning spots for lizards, and hiding places for mice and shrews. The rockery will also provide habitat for snails and slugs, but in the ideal wildlife garden, a balance will be achieved so that molluscs are not a serious pest. Pinks (*Dianthus*) are an attractive group which thrive in rockeries – and the native cheddar pink is widely available as seed.

Above: *Saxifrages are among the most popular of alpine plants and several species will thrive in rockeries, on walls and similar situations. The meadow saxifrage is a flower of old meadows.*

Below: *Although still common in botanic gardens, Alpine gardens are no longer as popular as in the 19th century. Alpines are characteristically small, low and dense, but also colourful.*

Ferneries

Ferneries were once a fashionable must for every Victorian gardener. However, they were responsible for the wholesale depletion of many fern species from the British countryside. In fact, some species have probably never recovered. Fortunately, for today's gardener, ferns are now propagated in nurseries.

A damp, north-facing wall is the ideal location for a fernery, and it is surprising how quickly it can be developed. By using plenty of bark mulch, as well as a few large slabs of bark between the plants, you can not only reduce the need for weeding, but also provide shelter for amphibians, which will also favour the fernery. Many ferns are surprisingly drought-resistant, and as they come in a wide range of sizes from the low-growing ferns, such as maidenhair, and even the hart's tongues and hard ferns, to the 2 m (6 ft) tall *Osmunda*, there is plenty of scope for variety. By combining logs with the fernery, and planting a few shade-loving exotic plants, such as *Trillium*, an interesting garden can be created. I have planted spring bulbs, such as snowdrop, snowflake and crocus in a fernery, as these are largely over before the ferns start spreading in spring. Creating a wildlife-friendly garden does not have to exclude conventional flower gardening.

Above: *The author's fernery forms a semi-natural boundary between the cultivated part of the garden, and a more natural area of woodland, where there is heavy shade.*

Above: *The royal fern is one of the largest species of native fern and popular with gardeners.* **Below:** *The maidenhair fern likes damp walls, but will thrive even on north-facing walls.*

Below: *Snowdrops have been widely cultivated, and many of those naturalized in gardens have their origins in as far away places as Turkey.*

Above: *The Crested Newt when on land is jet-black above with a bright yellow and black belly. It is a protected species in the UK, and its breeding ponds should not be disturbed.*

Above: *The Bogbean is one of many species of marshland plants with attractive flowers. If you have the space, a bog garden makes a very attractive addition to a wildlife garden.*

Wetlands

Even in a small garden, it is possible to create a wetland, and a pond can be extended into a bog garden, but it is in a larger garden that wetlands come into their own. A large pond with an extensive margin, planted with rushes, yellow flags, kingcups and other marginals, can provide habitat for a range of wildlife, and if the pond is big enough to have an expanse of bare mud, then migrating waders may pause for a day or two. In addition, any help that can be given the Water Vole, now in serious decline in Britain, is to be welcomed. With any wetland habitat it is important to provide plenty of shelter on land for amphibians, such as piles of logs, heaps of bricks, and anything else that will provide a humid, cool hiding place.

Below: *Generally only larger gardens have space for a bog, but if you have room, they can be really attractive to wildlife, as well as being colourful.*

Woodland glades

Many popular garden plants were originally found in woodland glades and the combination of trees, shade and open areas is both attractive to look at and good for a wide range of wildlife. Every naturalist will know that the greatest wildlife diversity is often found in woodland edges – hedgerows are to a greater extent continuous strips of woodland edge, which is why they are so important for so many species of wildlife. Also, the average suburban garden has many of the elements of woodland edge and its consequent diversity of species. Allowing a lawn to grow a few centimetres, rather than mowing down to a tennis-court height, will immediately increase the potential number of plant species. Many will colonize naturally, but others can be introduced. The more diverse the plants, the more diverse the other wildlife they will support. But, especially in rural areas, this will probably include mammals such as mice, voles and even Moles and Rabbits, which you may find are too destructive to tolerate.

Above: *A path through a woodland garden. Along woodland edges there is often a considerable variety of plants and wildlife. Hedgerows are in effect linear woodland edges.*

Left: *Bluebell woods, with their hazy blue carpets, are unique to Britain. Unfortunately, many of the bluebells sold in garden centres are the unscented, non-native, Spanish bluebell.*

The World Land Trust website explains some of the issues involved:

http//www.worldlandtrust.org/carbon/balance.htm

One simple solution is to practise permaculture and other low-tillage forms of gardening – using mulches. But even the latter have their energy implications – if you are using a plastic sheet mulch, how much energy was used to create it? How much energy was used in the supply chain to make bark chipping or aggregate mulches? Grass cuttings from a hand-propelled mower are among the best bets. But how many of us still use a hand-powered mower? Ride-on lawn mowers may be the most fun way of mowing the lawn, but they are not very efficient in terms of energy use.

Gardening and greenhouse gases

If you are reading this book you will almost certainly be interested in the conservation of the natural environment. You will also have a broad interest in conservation and other environmental issues. Therefore you should be aware of the overall environmental issues of gardening.

Greenhouse gases, particularly CO_2, are produced when we burn fossil fuels; this fact we are all aware of. What is not so well known is that farming and gardening also release large amounts of CO_2 into the atmosphere.

Facts and figures

- A Petrol lawnmower pollutes as much in an hour as 40 modern cars.
- A 3.5 hp mower emits the same amount of VOCs in an hour as a car driven for 340 miles.
- Agriculture is responsible for about a third of all greenhouse gases.

3

NOCTURNAL WILDLIFE

A host of nocturnal wildlife visits gardens, and after dark the garden can be just as interesting as during the day with species such as owls, mammals and moths making an appearance. Not only does attracting some species need patience, but for some luck is also needed.

Mammals at night

Most mammals are largely nocturnal and almost all are secretive. However, with protection from disturbance they often become relatively tame and easy to see. The nocturnal species can also be watched using red light, or by accustoming them to an ordinary floodlight.

Most mammals are not disturbed by red light. Using a red filter, it is possible to illuminate an area, such as a rockery, or a patch among bushes. Where they occur, Badgers and Foxes are relatively easy to induce to feed within a pool of light. To start with red light (a red filter placed over a light source) is less disturbing, but after a very short time, an ordinary floodlight will be tolerated. I have seen Badgers coming to floodlit patios in suburban London to feed on household scraps; they were so accustomed to humans that one walked over my feet while we were filming it.

With feeding stations similar to those used by birds, small mammals such as Wood Mice and Bank Voles can be attracted, and even shrews will visit to feed on mealworms. In fact, many bird tables are used at night by small mammals – Bank Voles, Wood Mice and rats. Perhaps the easiest of all to attract are Hedgehogs. A bowl of bread soaked in milk is the traditional food to put out for Hedgehogs, but they are omnivorous, and a good quality cat food, plus milk and raw egg is even more delectable to them. Food, such as pet food and household scraps, put out for Hedgehogs, Badgers and Foxes will generally attract smaller mammals such as Wood Mice as well. Also, of course, if they are around, it will attract rats.

Night time is a good time to view amphibians. Using a powerful torch, inspect your pond, as it is often

Above: *Bank Voles are surprisingly arboreal, climbing in hedges and bushes to feed on hips and haws and other fruits and berries.*

Opposite and below: *Badgers are normally strictly nocturnal, waiting until after sunset before emerging from the sett. The cubs follow their mother for the first few weeks after they venture above ground from the safety of their sett.*

Above: A Common Toad is the gardener's friend, feeding almost exclusively on slow-moving invertebrates, such as slugs. Toads will often live in a very limited area for several years, only moving away to mate in spring.

Below: A patio light will often attract huge numbers of insects, a phenomenon well known to entomologists.

Owls

Owls are more difficult to attract – they are all predators, and although they will occasionally take dead prey, they mostly feed on live mammals, birds and insects. So although it is possible to encourage owls to nest in a garden, generally speaking it is going to be a matter of luck if you see them at night.

much easier to see newts, frogs and toads after dark. You will probably be surprised to find them throughout the year. Despite what many books tell you, most amphibians are found in water almost any month of the year – I have found Great Crested Newts in the pond at Christmas time.

In the spotlight

Spotlighting for owls is good fun. With a powerful lamp (but not so bright as to cause blindness) it is possible to see owls, Foxes, deer, hares and other wildlife. You can either use a headlamp, or a hand-held torch – the latter is usually more powerful, but is also more cumbersome. However, it may not be a good idea to go 'lamping' in suburban areas. Even in rural areas you are liable to be stopped as a potential poacher.

Night-flying insects

Light pollution is a major problem, causing birds to become active in the middle of the night, and possibly causing migrants to become disorientated. Many naturalists would like to see a dramatic reduction in unnecessary street lighting. However, searching around external lights can provide a wealth of information on what moths and other nocturnal insects occur. Bats are often drawn to the insects flying around a lamp, and toads frequently learn that there is a ready supply of food fluttering around a light, and will wait for insects to fall to the ground. If you want to find out more about the night-flying moths and other insects, spread a sheet beneath a light and wait to see what turns up. The serious lepidopterist will use essentially the same technique – a more powerful mercury vapour lamp, with a high UV wave length.

For night-flying insects, it is important to ensure a supply of night-scented blossoms. Many white flowers are night-scented, and any gardener knows that certain species become much more powerfully scented as dusk approaches. And of course, just as sugar water, or

hummingbird feeders can be used for day-flying insects, they will also attract moths and other night-flying insects. Lepidopterists are familiar with 'sugaring'. Each person has their own favourite recipe for attracting moths – often a mixture of molasses, beer and treacle, spread on a post or tree. A good supply of insects is also a good way of attracting bats.

Above: *The Pine Marten is generally nocturnal, as it has been hunted for centuries. But where it is encouraged, it will visit feeders even by day.*

Below: *Hedgehogs are among the easiest of nocturnal wildlife to photograph, being relatively short-sighted they can be approached and snapped with an inexpensive instamatic.*

Hi-tech nocturnal wildlife watching

There is now a considerable array of lighting and other viewing equipment available, the only limitation being the depth of your pocket. Modern CCTV and web cams are a technological advance with great potential for wildlife viewing. Since much of the equipment is relatively cheap, it is becoming quite easy to adapt security systems for watching wildlife. Many modern systems will work at very low light intensities. Movement sensors, connected to a video or web cam to trigger recording, are potentially a very useful way of observing wildlife, even in the middle of the night. In this way, it is also possible to set up a web cam on the edge of a pond, sighted on some bait, and watch wildlife from the comfort of an armchair.

Many of the companies selling nest boxes now also sell equipment for viewing inside a nest box, and it is worth remembering that outside the breeding season this could be adapted for viewing small mammals.

4

FRIEND OR FOE?

Weeds and pests: how do you achieve a balance? It isn't always easy, and some wildlife that may be welcomed by one person constitutes a nuisance to another.

One of the problems with attracting wildlife is that not everyone is happy with all species. At the extreme end, most people agree that Brown Rats are undesirable – but even this species has its fans, notably TV naturalist Chris Packham. Magpies, crows, Sparrowhawks, deer, Grey Squirrels and Rabbits all have their admirers as well as detractors. But in most cases, if you don't want these species, it is relatively easy to take measures to keep them at bay. Placing feeders inside a 'cage' of wide mesh that allows small birds to fly in and out, is a very effective way of keeping Magpies and crows away, while fences can be used to keep out Rabbits, hares and deer.

Weeds

It is a platitude that weeds are a flower in the wrong place, and this is particularly true when gardening for wildlife. Some plants that would be considered quite out of place in a conventional garden become attractive additions to a wildlife garden. Thistles are a particularly good example. Apart from the Scottish thistle and a few other species, most are regarded as weeds in the majority of gardens. However, they are particularly attractive to Goldfinches and, when cultivated, many species are extremely pretty 'architectural' plants. Brambles are a

Above: *Squirrels, such as this Red Squirrel, are easily attracted to feeders, but many people resent squirrels, particularly Grey Squirrels, because they are greedy eaters.*

Opposite: *A Heron showing why it can be unpopular in gardens. In large gardens predation by Herons can be tolerated, but in small gardens it is easy to stop them taking fish and amphibians.*

Below: *Blackberries. Despite their ability to become invasive, they are a splendid plant for any wildlife garden.*

Below: *Ragwort is the food plant for Cinnabar Moths. But it is highly toxic to livestock and must not stray into hay crops.*

herbicides are non-persistent, and rapidly biodegrade. Where there is a particular problem in a garden, it may in some circumstances be preferable to spot kill the weeds, as this will cause less damage to the environment than digging it all over. But I can see very little justification for ever using insecticides. There is such an acute shortage of all types of insects that even pest species have their benefits for a wide range of wildlife. If insecticides have to be used, they should normally be pyrethrum-based, but remember even though these are not toxic to mammals, they are extremely toxic if they get into ponds and streams.

weed only when out of control, and if they are pruned heavily each year, they will provide both dense cover for a wide range of wildlife and safe breeding places for several species of birds. Additionally, you can share their abundant supply of autumn fruits with the wildlife.

Although there is no substitute for hand weeding, there is sometimes a case for the carefully controlled selective use of certain herbicides. Some systemic

Above: *A pond with wires around it, which will prevent Herons gaining access to the pond.*

Below: *Koi Carp are popular with many gardeners, but like most fish are not conducive to wildlife, particularly amphibians, whose eggs and larvae the fish eat.*

Fish

In a wildlife-friendly garden the general advice about fish is: none. Fish are generally destructive to amphibians as they eat amphibian eggs and larvae. However, you may well want to have some ornamental fish, such as Koi or Goldfish. The best solution is probably to have two ponds: one an ornamental pond for fish, and the other a more natural pond for other wildlife. The former can be kept Heron and cat proof. Screens are essential if you are to keep all predators away from ponds, but if Herons are the only serious threat, they can be deterred by erecting a 'fence' of thread or wire around the pond close to the water's edge. Since Herons settle on dry land and walk to the water, this prevents them gaining access. If you are going to keep fish, then how about native species? However, sources of native fish are very few, and I certainly would not want to encourage taking them from the wild. Consult the nature conservation authorities, or your local wildlife conservation trust (*see* page 156) for advice.

Making your pets wildlife friendly

Cats and dogs

For the wildlife-friendly garden, neither cats nor dogs are the ideal occupants, but the fact is that a large number of people who like wildlife also like cats and dogs. Dogs frighten wildlife away, and while certain dogs will chase birds, Rabbits and hares, most are ineffectual as predators. The same is not true of cats. Before I go any further, I should make it quite clear that I am not anti pets. I have dogs and a wide range of other pets. From earliest childhood, I have lived in houses where cats are an integral part of the family. But if I had my way, cats would not be allowed out of the house off a lead. There are estimated to be some 7 million pet cats in the United Kingdom, and if those cats take an average of one item of wildlife prey a week – a lot for some, but not much for many others – they kill some 364 million creatures a year. On top of that there are an estimated one million feral cats, which are probably killing at least 10 animals a week each – another 500 million animals. So it is probably safe to say that cats are responsible for the demise of at least 500 million birds and animals a year, possibly as many as one billion. For many species of wildlife this is too much. Studies in North America suggest that for some bird populations, cat predation could be the ultimate factor in their demise. The local extinction of Common Lizards can probably be attributed to cat predation in England.

It is not necessary for cats to go roaming gardens. The average house or flat gives them ample space to exercise. There is nothing cruel in this, cats are essentially lazy, so provided they are well fed, and get plenty of exercise, they will not miss killing wildlife. It is purely to justify our sentimental view of animals that we allow them to run free in gardens and the countryside (where they usually run a serious risk of being killed crossing a road, as well as being exposed to numerous other hazards). Ideally, a wildlife-friendly garden will not have cats and dogs roaming at will.

When I grew up in suburban London in the late 1940s and early 1950s, most dog owners used to let their dogs roam the streets each evening. Not only were they a road hazard, but they also fouled footpaths and gardens – something very few people would consider tolerating nowadays. So why do we condone cats roaming and killing wildlife?

However, until legislation is introduced making it illegal to let cats roam free, we have to find other means of protecting birds and other wildlife from their depredations. Bells are a small help, and it is sometimes claimed that two bells are better than one. An increasing number of electronic anti-predator devices are available. There are also sprays and other deterrents,

Above: *Cats are undoubtedly the most significant mammalian predators on wildlife, particularly in towns and suburbs. However, in the countryside there are often many Feral Cats.*

but it is difficult to ascertain which are effective. The RSPB is actively researching ways of deterring cats, and up-to-date reports of successful trials are posted on the Society's website (*see* page 156).

Handling wild animals

While the risk of disease is generally low, it should always be borne in mind that animals that are easy to catch are often sick or injured, and therefore are more likely to be carrying disease. Although the threat of disease such as rabies is also extremely low, there are numerous other diseases that are carried, particularly by mammals and birds, and some are transmittable to humans. If you do need to handle a sick or injured mammal or bird you should always wear gloves.

Mammals

SPECIES	FRIEND	FOE	SOLUTIONS
Bats	Yes, prey on insects	Occasionally causes problems with accumulation of droppings and urine	Consult statutory nature authorities and exclude
Mole	In very large gardens helps maintain soil structure	Yes, ruins lawn	Exclusion by burying wire netting
Hedgehog	Yes, preys on slugs and snails and other invertebrates	Occasionally, may attack ground-nesting birds	Difficult, best tolerated
House Mouse	Rarely	Normally yes, extensive damage to stored food and property	Trapping, or in severe infestations, poisoning with care
Wood Mouse	Normally yes, important prey for owls	Occasionally damages stored food	Live trap and release away from house
Brown Rat	Rarely	Normally yes, extensive damage to stored food and property	As with the House Mouse, but generally easier to exclude
Voles	Normally yes, important prey for owls	Can do damage to roots	Tolerate, it is normally a short-term problem
Squirrels	Generally yes, attractive and entertaining	Can predate small birds; over enthusiastic feeder at bird tables	Ensure safe site for nest boxes; use squirrel-proof feeders
Rabbit	Sometimes, but only in very large gardens	Yes, in smaller gardens, causes extensive damage	Exclude with wire netting
Weasels and Stoats	Generally yes, since they only occur rarely	Can do damage to pets	Exclude from pets such as Guinea Pigs, Rabbits and Chickens by ensuring their cages have small wire mesh
Fox	Generally yes, since they are mostly scavengers around the garden	Can predate pets and livestock	Ensure Chickens, ducks etc are locked away at night
Feral Cats	No	Generally yes, major predator of wildlife	Difficult, trapping and neutering
Deer	Only in large gardens	Yes, in small gardens, can do serious damage	Exclude with high fences, or even an electric fence

Below: *Moles are interesting mammals, but few gardeners can tolerate the damaging molehills or 'tumps' which their activities produce.*

The definition of friend or foe for mammals is complex. Generally most mammals have been perceived as pests, but with a more tolerant attitude to wildlife most have been 'rehabilitated'. However, in a conventional suburban garden, larger species, such as Rabbits and deer, can do an immense amount of damage in a very short space of time and there are very few circumstances where House Mice and Brown Rats can be tolerated. In most cases, if an animal does become a pest then specialist advice will be needed, because there are also animal welfare issues to consider. It is all very well trapping a Feral Cat that is ravaging the wildlife in your garden – but what to do with it then? It is best to consult with nature authorities or the RSPCA (*see* page 156).

The above table gives a very simplified summary of the options available to the gardener.

Birds

SPECIES	FRIEND	FOE	SOLUTIONS
Heron	Only in large gardens	A problem with fishponds	Exclude with cotton treads around the pond, or cover with netting
Ducks	Only in large gardens	Rarely	Put netting over ponds
Moorhen	Normally, yes	Can be a pest in large numbers	Exclude from feeding areas
Sparrowhawk	Normally, yes	Predates tits and other small birds	Tolerate, site feeding areas to reduce predation
Pheasant	Normally, yes	Can damage gardens when present in large numbers	Exclude from feed
Great Spotted Woodpecker	Yes	Can damage nest boxes and predate birds	Protect the boxes with hole guards
Pigeons	Normally, yes	Only a problem in large numbers	Exclude from feed
Magpies	Normally, yes	Perceived as a threat to small birds	Tolerate, but ensure nest boxes are safe from them
Crows	Normally, yes	Perceived as a threat to small birds	Tolerate, but ensure nest boxes are safe from them
Jay	Normally, yes	Perceived as a threat to small birds	Tolerate, but ensure nest boxes are safe from them
Starling	Normally, yes	Greedy, but not a threat to other wildlife	Provide starling-proof feeders, if large numbers are present
House Sparrow	Normally, yes	Greedy, but not a threat to other wildlife	Encourage, numbers have plummeted

Birds are generally seen in a positive way by most gardeners, with Robins, Blue Tits, Chaffinches and other species almost universally popular. However, a few species present problems, particularly those that do predate other birds. Someone feeding Blue Tits might find it hard to accept a Sparrowhawk dashing through their garden once a day or more and grabbing a tit to eat. But just as naturalists spent a long time arguing that gamekeepers were wrong to persecute everything with a hooked beak, we should be aware that this is part of a balanced ecosystem, however distressing it is at the time. Just remember that predation on wildlife in gardens by other birds is part of a more or less natural ecosystem, but the real damage is done by the hundreds of thousands of pet cats that kill a few birds, and then retire to sleep for another 23 hours in front of the fire. If you have a problem with predation by Magpies or other birds, try to put it in perspective of a balanced environment, and if the problem persists, try to take measures that protect the prey – it is rarely necessary to persecute the predators.

Right: *A male Starling singing. It is a mimic often copying the sounds of other birds and even telephones.*

Amphibians, Reptiles and Invertebrates

SPECIES	FRIEND	FOE	SOLUTIONS
Grass Snake	Yes	Can sometimes predate fish	Encourage, seriously declining in most areas
Adder	Generally, no	Mostly unpopular as it is venomous	Rare in gardens, consult nature authorities if they are present
Slow Worm	Yes	No	Encourage, declining in most areas
Frogs	Normally, yes	Can cause problems by strangling Goldfish	Remove fish and encourage wildlife
Toads	Normally, yes	Can cause problems by strangling Goldfish	Remove fish and encourage wildlife
Moths	In garden, yes	Some species cause problems	Exclude from houses by closing windows, or using insect screens
Wood-boring beetles	In garden, yes	Serious pest to property	Keep houses dry, and use environmentally benign insecticides
Aphids	In small numbers, yes	In large numbers, yes	Encourage natural predators such as ladybirds and small birds
Slugs and snails	In moderate numbers, yes	In excessive numbers, yes	Encourage natural predators such as Hedgehogs and Slow Worms
Other invertebrates	Generally, yes	In excessive numbers, generally yes	Develop an ecologically balanced garden

This table includes many of the traditional garden pests, plus a few animals often persecuted quite senselessly. With many species in serious decline or even locally extinct, it is important to protect as many as possible. In the early 21st century it is almost impossible to appreciate the huge numbers of insects and other species that once populated our towns and suburbs. Their decline has lead to a catastrophic decline in the numbers of many species of birds, bats and other wildlife. Unless a species can be shown to be causing actual and serious damage, a wildlife gardener should always err on the side of caution, tolerate, or encourage.

Below: *Two-spot Ladybird. Ladybirds prey on aphids, and they can be encouraged by providing shelter for them.*

Below: *A Song Thrush smashing a snail on its 'anvil'. Snail remains often litter the area around a suitable rock or brick.*

Weeds

SPECIES	FRIEND	FOE	SOLUTIONS
Nettles	Yes, in moderation	Can take over	Control by pulling up by roots or mowing large areas 2-3 times a year
Grasses	Yes	Some species become a pest in conventional flower-beds	Hand weed
Dock	Yes, if you have the space	Only in flower gardens	Hand weed with a spade
Thistles	Definitely yes, if you have the space	A problem in a small garden	Hand weed with a spade
Brambles	Definitely yes, if you have the space	Very invasive	Use cultivated varieties, and hand prune wild ones
Blackthorn	Yes	Suckers can be a problem	Dig out annually; never spray as this may kill the hedge
Elder	Yes	Often unpopular, with many superstitions relating to it	Encourage, good for birds and insects
Bindweed	Yes, provides cover	Can take over	Hand weed, easily controlled; originally introduced as a garden flower in northern Europe
Fat hen	Yes, important food for many birds	Only in vegetable gardens	Tolerate
Giant Hogweed	No	Sap can cause skin blisters	An exotic species that only really has a place in very large gardens
Plantains	Yes	Disliked by gardeners	Tolerate, seeds are good for wildlife
Ragwort	In small numbers, yes	In pasture yes, as poisonous to cattle and horses	Tolerate in small numbers in appropriate places only
Groundsel	Yes	Only in formal gardens	Tolerate, much liked by birds
Other 'weeds'	Generally, yes	Only when out of control	Tolerate as wide a variety as possible, within the constraints

Weeds: Friend or Foe? A weed is defined as a plant in the wrong place, and in the wildlife garden many weeds are highly desirable. A small selection of plants considered weeds are tabulated as examples. In general, it depends on the size of the garden as to how many 'weeds' can be tolerated. If you have a large garden, then you should encourage as many as possible of the rare species of so-called weeds, and some of the books (see page 158) will advise on suitable species.

Right: *Nettles may have painful stings and are generally considered a weed, but if there is space in a garden they should be tolerated, as they are foodplants for several caterpillars, but need to be in full sunlight for most butterflies.*

5

DIRECTORY OF GARDEN SPECIES

By managing a garden sympathetically a wide range of wildlife can be attracted. The species that will arrive and feed or make their homes will vary depending on the surrounding habitats. The various mammals, birds, amphibians, reptiles and insects shown on the following pages are just a small selection of the wildlife that you may encounter in any garden.

Mammals p66
There are about 150 land mammals in Europe. The largest animals to visit the garden, they are not often seen as most of them are nocturnal.

Birds p90
The most familiar animal to be seen in the garden, the addition of a pond and feeders is an excellent way of attracting a wide variety.

Amphibians and Reptiles p132
Northern Europe have less species due to the climate. Amphibians and reptiles cannot survive very cold conditions and hibernate. In some northern European countries this can be for two-thirds of the year.

Insects p138
Ranging from beetles to butterflies, not only are insects and other invertebrates attractive and in some cases beneficial additions to a wildlife garden, they are also a valuable source of food for mammals, birds, amphibians and reptiles.

Opposite: *Starling numbers in northern Europe are augmented in winter by the arrival of many birds migrating from Russia. Rotting apples provide food for them as well as migrant thrush species.*

Below: *The Dormouse is rare in gardens, but it will enter sheds and lofts in search of food. If you live in the right area, and plant hazel, they may be attracted.*

BATS

Bats are the only mammals capable of true flight. All the species found in Europe feed mostly on flying insects, although some pick grubs and spiders off trees, and some take fish occasionally. They all use echo location to find their way, having very poor eyesight. All bats are protected by law in the UK, and if you find a colony you must not disturb it without consulting with the nature conservation authorities. Bats can be encouraged by openings in roof timbers to allow access to roof spaces (but ensure these areas are free of any harmful timber treatment pesticides). Although a bat conservationist recently died of a rabies-like virus, caught from a bat bite, the risks are actually extremely low. However, bats (or any other wild mammal) should never be handled without wearing gloves.

Common Pipistrelle
Pipistrellus pipistrellus

Identification
The smallest European bat, measuring 32–51 mm (1.25–2 in) long, and with a wingspan of up to 24 cm (10 in). Until recently only one species of Common Pipistrelle was known but in the 1990s a second species was discovered in England. It is known as the Soprano Pipistrelle.

In the Garden
Pipistrelles commonly roost in roofs, but are difficult to find as they hide in very small crevices. Bats prefer clean dust-free environments, and so they are often attracted to roost in the roofs of houses on new estates. They will use bat boxes.

Breeding
One or two young, born naked and helpless, carried by the mother until too heavy, when they are left in the nursery roost.

Above: *The Serotine is one of the larger European bats, and often roosts in the roof space of houses.*

Feeding
They feed exclusively on flying insects – so a pesticide-free garden is the best way of encouraging them.

Left: *Bats can squeeze into remarkably small holes, and a bat box can contain up to 50 or more Pipistrelles. Boxes should be draught-free, and thick enough to provide protection from extremes of temperature.*

Serotine *Eptesicus serotinus*

Identification
A large bat that is often found roosting in houses. It has a body length of 82 mm (3 in) and a wingspan of up to 38 cm (15 in). It is dark brown, with broad wings.

In the Garden
Widespread in northern Europe, as far north as central England and Denmark. It often roosts in buildings in rural and suburban areas.

Breeding
Has a single young, born naked and helpless, at first carried by the mother.

Feeding
Feeds exclusively on insects, including larger species such as beetles.

Greater Horseshoe Bat
Rhinolophus ferrumequinum

Identification
A large and distinctive bat, up to 11 cm (4.5 in) long and with a wingspan of up to 40 cm (16 in), and with a characteristic horseshoe-shaped appendage on the nose.

In the Garden
Although now considerably reduced in numbers, and largely confined to the west of England and Wales, it is a species that often occurs in houses, churches, barns and also cellars and tunnels. However, since it is seriously endangered, it should be disturbed as little as possible, and if you do find them, the nature authorities should be notified.

Above: Long-eared Bats often roost in clusters, hanging free from the ceiling. When the bats are torpid, the ears are curled and not obvious, until they become active and unfurl them.

Breeding
The females gather in nursery colonies, of up to 200 females, in church towers, attics and barn roofs. They have a single young.

Feeding
Exclusively insects and spiders, often hovering to pick insects off tree leaves.

Brown Long-eared Bat *Plecotus auritus*

Identification
A very distinctive bat with huge ears, up to 4 cm (1.6 in) long, and a total body length of only 55 mm (2 in). Its wingspan is 42 cm (16.5 in). The huge ears are curled up when it is at rest.

In the Garden
One of the bats most commonly found roosting in houses and feeding in gardens. When Brown Long-eared Bats roost in attics they are often found hanging free or against a wall near the top of the roof space. They will also roost in bat boxes. Their flight is fairly slow, and they often hover, picking insects off trees.

Breeding
A single young (occasionally two), born naked and helpless, and carried by the mother for the first few days. They are mature at 1–2 years.

Feeding
They feed on insects and spiders, caught on the wing.

Below: Once widespread and common in roofs, church towers and cellars, the Greater Horseshoe Bat is now endangered.

SHREWS

Shrews are insectivores, similar in size to mice. They have very simple peg-like teeth, very small eyes and ears largely hidden in their fur. They are active in short bursts, 24 hours of the day, consuming about their own weight in food every day. They feed on grubs, worms, molluscs and other invertebrates, but they will also prey on baby mice and voles should the opportunity arise. Most shrews are relatively short-lived, with those born in late summer surviving to the following spring, but very few living much more than a year. They are preyed on by a wide variety of raptors. Some mammals – notably domestic cats - will often kill them, but find them distasteful and do not eat them.

Common Shrew *Sorex araneus*

Identification
As its name suggests, this is generally the most frequently encountered shrew. It has a total length of about 125 mm (5 in) including the tail, which is up to 47 mm (nearly 2 in) and is proportionally shorter than that of the Pygmy Shrew. It is usually a chocolate-brown above, whitish grey below. Its high-pitched squeaking can often be heard in hedgerows, although the human ability to hear the high frequency declines with age.

In the Garden
Common Shrews live in the runs and tunnels of other small mammals, and they can be encouraged to make their nests under boards, corrugated iron and logs. Shrews are often killed by cats, but they are distasteful and, therefore, rarely eaten. However, they are eaten by Barn Owls and other birds of prey.

Breeding
Up to 5 litters a year, in a nest of grass, under a log, sheet of corrugated iron, or in a burrow. There are usually 5–7 young in a litter, which are born naked, blind and helpless.

Feeding
Insects, earthworms and other invertebrates. Occasionally other small animals.

Above: *A Common Shrew showing its characteristic, long pointed snout. The teeth are in a simple peg-like row and become worn down during their lifetime, which is a factor influencing its relatively short life – very few survive more than a year.*

Left: *A Common Shrew, with characteristic chocolate-brown, velvety fur. Shrews are frequently heard squeaking in hedgerows, but are rarely seen, as they spend most of their life in tunnels, or thick vegetation.*

Above: *A Pygmy Shrew. This shrew is found throughout the British isles and has even been recorded near the summit of Ben Nevis.*

Pygmy Shrew *Sorex minutus*

Identification
A very small brownish shrew, with a total length of under 105 mm (4 in), which can also be distinguished from the Common Shrew by its proportionally longer tail, which is nearly half the body's total length.

In the Garden
Although generally less numerous than the Common Shrew, the Pygmy is more widespread. It can be encouraged in the same way as for Common Shrews. Pygmy Shrews are also not uncommon in bird boxes, and it is likely that they are more arboreal than is often realized.

Breeding
They have up to 4 litters a year, in a grass-lined nest, underground, in a hollow, log, or similar situation. The litter contains up to 12 young, which are born naked, blind and helpless.

Feeding
Exclusively on live prey, particularly insect grubs, earthworms and other invertebrates.

Water Shrew *Neomys fodiens*

Identification
This is a relatively large shrew, growing to a total length of nearly 15 cm (6 in), of which the tail is up to 74 mm (3 in). It is black above, and silvery white below, and the feet and tail have fringes of stiff hairs to assist it swimming. When it dives, it appears silvery from the air trapped in its fur.

In the Garden
Despite the name, Water Shrews can often be found some distance from water. Nonetheless, they are most often encountered near ponds and streams. They rarely stay in water for long, but emerge into tunnels, and as they push through the tunnels, the water is squeezed from their fur. They can also be found under planks and corrugated iron placed near water.

Breeding
They have 2-3 litters a year of 3-9 young, born naked and helpless, that are mature when 2-3 months old.

Feeding
They feed on small fish as well as almost any other small animal they can capture.

Below: *The Water Shrew is the largest of the shrews found in Britain, and normally only seen as it swims and dives.*

69

HEDGEHOG AND MOLE

These are two of the larger insectivores and in continental Europe there are several species of mole and three species of hedgehog. Hedgehogs are particularly abundant in suburban habitats, where they are valued as the gardener's friend, because they eat so many slugs and snails. Moles are rather the reverse – the gardener's enemy, because of their disturbance to lawns.

Hedgehog *Erinaceus europaeus*

Identification
One of the most popular of garden mammals, it is also one of the most distinctive, growing to a total length of up to 30 cm (12 in). The Hedgehog's fur is mostly modified into sharp spines, but the underside is softer. Unfortunately, their spines make it almost impossible for Hedgehogs to groom efficiently and consequently they are frequently infested with fleas and other parasites. They are also prone to infestations of greenbottle fly larvae, which burrow into the nostrils, and often cause the Hedgehogs to become disorientated.

In the Garden
Hedgehogs have adapted very successfully to garden habitats. They are particularly numerous in suburban areas and, despite heavy mortality on roads, are generally flourishing. Hedgehogs are easy to attract – the commonest way is a dish of milk; added cat food will be welcome and despite the fact that most people think they have one regular visitor, very often it is several Hedgehogs calling in succession. Also, in late summer expect to see the young ones. Hedgehog nest boxes can

Above: *Hedgehogs can readily be attracted to gardens by leaving out bowls of milk, with dog biscuit or bread soaked in it. Place it where light from a window or a garden light falls.*

Below: *Hedgehogs are normally nocturnal. If they are seen in broad daylight, it is often because they are injured or sick. A common problem is infestation with Greenbottle Fly maggots.*

be purchased, but a good brush pile next to a compost heap is probably just as good. Or you could make a chamber with bricks and a paving slab. Be careful when dismantling a compost heap, particularly if you are using a fork and do remember to check any bonfires that have been left for a few days, in case a Hedgehog has taken up residence. Despite their rather ungainly appearance, Hedgehogs are remarkably agile; they can run quite fast, are good climbers and can swim. However, they do drown even in small ponds, if they cannot climb out, so remember to have plenty of ways of escape. If you have water butts, keep them covered - they can be death traps for Hedgehogs and other wildlife.

Breeding
They have one or two litters of up to 5 young, born helpless with only a few, soft spines. They make their nest in thick cover, often in compost heaps. Hedgehogs born late in the year often do not survive hibernation – they need to weigh about 400 g (14 oz) when they commence hibernation.

Feeding
Hedgehogs feed mostly on earthworms, slugs, grubs and other invertebrates, but they will also eat baby mice, birds' eggs, amphibians and carrion. In addition to milk, they will enjoy mealworms and some petshops sell canned food especially for Hedgehogs.

Mole *Talpa europaea*

Identification
Although rarely seen, the Mole is easily recognized by its velvety jet-black fur, pointed snout, large forepaws and virtually no sign of ears or eyes. It grows to about 15 cm (6 in) and has a tiny tail, less than 4 cm (1.5 in) long.

In the Garden
Unless the garden is large, Moles are generally not popular, because of their extensive tunneling, and the heaps of soil they throw up (tumps, or molehills). There are lots of remedies for this, ranging from electronic devices alleged to scare Moles away, to placing mothballs in their runs. However, none are proven to be 100% successful. The Mole hunts by crawling through its tunnels and searching for any worms or other invertebrates that have fallen in. Consequently, if the runs are flattened (with a roller), it simply encourages the mole to dig even more. Before the days of potting compost, gardeners used to gather the soil of molehills to use in seed trays. Moles help to maintain the drainage and fertility of the soil.

Breeding
One litter of 3 or 4 blind, naked young, born in an underground nest.

Feeding
Almost exclusively earthworms and insect grubs.

Below: *Moles are rarely seen above ground. However, if you notice the soil moving, and stand patiently, you may be rewarded with a glimpse of one, as in this photo.*

Above: *Moles feed extensively on earthworms, but they will also eat almost any other invertebrate that happens to fall into their tunnels.*

RATS AND MICE

A few species of rats and mice can be serious pests, causing millions of pounds worth of damage each year. They are readily attracted to gardens, and although not always a desirable inclusion to the garden wildlife, their presence is unavoidable. The rat that spread the plagues that devastated Europe in the Middle Ages was the Black Rat, which is now almost extinct over most of northern Europe. The Black Rat was displaced in the 18th century by the Brown Rat. Although generally only found in the garden or hedgerows, both the Yellow-necked and the Wood Mouse often come into houses, particularly at the beginning of winter. They can do just as much damage to stored foods as the House Mouse. They can be attracted to feeding tables, with mixed seeds, nuts and berries. They are active all the year round, but tend to live in runs beneath the ground when there is snow cover. They can be encouraged in gardens by planting shrubs, bushes and other food plants, and also by creating brush and log piles to provide shelter, and also by planting hedges.

Above: Brown Rats are found in almost every habitat, from urban sewers to rural hedgerows. Although they are largely terrestrial, they are often seen swimming.

Below: Brown Rats feed on almost anything that might be considered edible. They are nest predators, taking eggs and also baby birds, and will raid hen houses for eggs.

Brown Rat *Rattus norvegicus*

Identification
A large rodent growing to a total length of up to 45 cm (17 in), of which the tail is over half. The colour is generally brownish, but it is rather variable. It has a characteristic 'greasy' appearance. When swimming the Brown Rat can be distinguished from the rarer Water Vole by its much longer, tapering tail.

In the Garden
Widespread and often all too common, particularly in rural areas. Brown Rats are agile climbers and swimmers, and when attracting wildlife by putting out food it is very important not to encourage Brown Rats. At the first sign of them, you should cease putting out food where they can reach it, and if there is any evidence of damage notify local pest control officers. Unless trained, it is unwise to set traps or put down poisons, as you may well end up killing other species of wildlife. It is a pity that rats are so destructive, since they are intelligent, and their antics to get at bird feeders can be very amusing. Dead or dying rats should never be handled with bare hands.

Breeding
The Brown Rat is very prolific, having 5 litters a year of up to 15 young (usually 7 or 8), born naked and helpless. The young are capable of breeding when only 3–4 months old.

Feeding
Brown Rats are true omnivores and they will eat almost anything including cereal packets as well as the contents – a reason for their prevalence.

House Mouse *Mus domesticus*

Identification
It is small, up to 18 cm (7 in) long, of which the tail is over half. It is generally a 'mousy', greyish brown colour, with small eyes and a fairly pointed muzzle. The first sign of their presence in a house is usually their small elongate black droppings, and their characteristic odour. In fact, there are several species of House Mouse found in Europe, all very similar, and only distinguishable by an expert. The one occurring in Britain is the Western House Mouse.

In the Garden
Likely to occur in any garden, but usually close to houses or sheds. The House Mouse is a true commensal, always being associated with human habitations. The island of St Kilda in the Hebrides was evacuated in the 1930s, and at the time a distinct subspecies of House Mouse occurred commonly on the island, but shortly after the evacuation, it became extinct.

Breeding
They can have up to 10 litters a year, with each litter containing up to 9 or more young, and the young are old enough to reproduce when only 6 weeks old. As infestations can be built up rapidly, it is important to eradicate them as soon as their presence is detected.

Above: *Baby House Mice are born naked, blind and helpless, in a nest lined with fur, hair, feathers and other soft materials. They will be rearing their own young in about a month after they have left the nest.*

Feeding
House Mice will feed on almost anything, and can live for long periods without water, metabolizing water from their food. They have been known to live and breed in cold stores.

Below: *House Mice do enormous amounts of damage to stored foods, and have even been known to live in refrigerated meat stores. Infestations have a characteristic odour.*

Wood Mouse *Apodemus sylvaticus*

Identification

Also known as the Long-tailed Field Mouse, it is easily distinguished from the House Mouse by its slightly larger size (head and body up to 11 cm (4 in), and a tail of equal length) more brown colouring, longer tail and large ears and eyes. The Wood Mouse also jumps in a characteristically erratic manner, whereas the House Mouse scurries close to the ground.

In the Garden

Wood Mice are agile climbers and often use old birds' nests, such as those of a Song Thrush or Blackbird, as feeding tables, where huge quantities of hawthorn berry skins and other detritus accumulate. They can be encouraged to nest under sheets of corrugated iron, planks. and logs. They will also be attracted to nest boxes which are placed low in bushes or on the ground. The Wood Mouse is an important item of prey for owls.

Breeding

Wood Mice breed in underground nests, but they will also nest under iron sheets, and in nest boxes; they have 3 or 4 litters of 3–9 young, which are born blind and naked.

Feeding

They feed on a wide range of seeds, fruits and other vegetable matter, and also invertebrates such as insect grubs and molluscs. Wood Mice will take a wide variety of seeds and nuts as well as mealworms at a feeding table.

Below: *Like many other small mammals, Wood Mice find blackberries a very attractive food in the late summer. It is always worth growing a few brambles for wildlife.*

Above: *The Wood Mouse is best identified by its yellowish-brown colouring, large eyes and large ears. The House Mouse is always greyer.*

Above: *The Yellow-necked Mouse is very similar to the Wood Mouse, but is slightly larger, and has a yellow band across the chest. It is less widespread, but not rare.*

Yellow-necked Mouse
Apodemus flavicollis

Identification
A larger version of the Wood Mouse of up to 13 cm (5 in), plus a tail of equal length, it has a characteristic yellowish-fawn band across the chest.

In the Garden
The Yellow-necked Mouse is not as widely distributed as the Wood Mouse, being most common across southern England. However, even within its range its distribution is patchy. Its habits are very similar to those of the Wood Mouse, but it is possibly even more arboreal, and often found in roofs and attics. For such a small mammal the Yellow-necked Mouse can be surprisingly noisy.

Breeding
Three litters of 2–9 young, born naked and helpless, which mature in 2–3 months.

Feeding
Very similar to the Wood Mouse, feeding on a wide range of mostly plant food.

Harvest Mouse *Micromys minutus*

Identification
The smallest mouse, weighing in at only 3.5–13 g (0.1–0.5 oz), and with a body length of 5–7.8 cm (2–3 in). The 4–7.5 cm, (1.5-2.8 in) tail is prehensile. It is usually slower moving than other mice. The colouring is often a relatively bright orange-brown.

In the Garden
Although Harvest Mice are traditionally associated with fields of corn, modern agricultural methods have largely eliminated them from this habitat, and they are now most often found in reed beds and hedgerows, but are also likely to turn up in gardens in rural areas. Harvest Mice build cricket-ball sized nests woven from grasses, which are often fairly obvious in autumn when vegetation has died down. They can also be found under iron sheets, and other similar coverings.

Breeding
They have up to 7 litters a year of 3–7 young, born naked and helpless, which mature in about 6 weeks.

Feeding
Mostly seeds, insects and other small invertebrates.

Below: *The diminutive Harvest Mouse was first noticed in Britain by Gilbert White, the 18th-century parson-naturalist of Selborne. It is fairly widespread, but easily overlooked.*

VOLES

Voles are small rodents, blunt-headed, with tails shorter than the body. They only rarely come into houses. They are often very numerous, and some species are cyclical (like Lemmings) building to a very high population density, and then crashing.

Above: *The Bank Vole is common in hedgerows and embankments as its name suggests, but it is also a surprisingly good climber, and is occasionally found in bird boxes.*

Below: *Rose hips are popular food for many small rodents, and the remains are often found under logs, sheets of iron and other places where they nest.*

Bank Vole *Clethrionomys glareolus*

Identification
Small, with a total length of up to 12 cm (4.7 in), of which the tail is about half, with a reddish brown tinge to the fur, and ears that are just visible.

In the Garden
The Bank Vole is widespread over much of Europe including Britain, and was introduced into Ireland where its range is still spreading. It is common in hedgerows, woodlands and similar habitats, including gardens in rural areas. It is secretive and partly nocturnal, and an agile climber, climbing in hedges and trees. It will sometimes use bird boxes when they are not occupied. Bank Voles create a network of surface tunnels, and build a nest of fine grasses and roots. If present in a garden, they can readily be encouraged to nest under sheets of corrugated iron, planks or logs.

Breeding
They have up to 4 litters a year, of up to 6 young, born in a nest usually lined with finely shredded grasses. The young are born naked and helpless, and are mature at about 4–5 weeks.

Feeding
Although Bank Voles feed mostly on plant matter, including seeds, nuts, berries and other fruits, they also feed on a wide range of invertebrates, and they often clamber in hedges, consuming nuts and berries. They can be attracted to feeding stations, and observed at night with a red light.

Short-tailed Vole
Microtus agrestis

Identification
Also known as the Field Vole – a tautology as vole is derived from a word meaning field – it is greyish brown, with a short tail and ears almost entirely concealed in its fur. It has a total length of up to 14 cm (5.5 in), of which the tail is less than 5 cm (2 in).

In the Garden
It is primarily a mammal of open grasslands and pastures, but, in rural areas, will readily occupy gardens, provided the grass is long enough for it to build its network of surface and subterranean runs.

Breeding
Short-tailed Voles are easily encouraged to make their nests and runs under sheets of corrugated iron, boards, or logs. The nest is usually made from finely shredded grasses and there are up to 6 litters a year of 4–6 young which are mature at about 3 weeks. In some areas the populations are cyclic, building up and then crashing.

Feeding
They feed mostly on roots and grasses.

Above: *The Short-tailed Vole is primarily found in grassy habitats. It makes tunnels among the grasses, or just below ground and feeds on roots as well as grass stems.*

Below: *Water Voles were once common and widespread in Britain, often occurring in larger gardens with ponds. However, in the latter part of the 20th century their numbers crashed.*

Water Vole *Arvicola terrestris*

Identification
The largest vole, the Water Vole grows to a total length of about 30 cm (12 in), of which the tail is about 13 cm (5 in). It is dark brown, blackish or dark reddish brown.

In the Garden
Only likely to occur in gardens with ponds or a stream and increasingly rare. Its decline is assumed to be a direct result of the spread of Mink, as it is easy prey.

Breeding
Water Voles have 3–4 litters a year of 3–6 young, born naked and helpless in a burrow. They are mature at about 4–5 weeks.

Feeding
Although they feed primarily on aquatic vegetation, grasses and roots, they also feed on fish, carrion and other small animals.

DORMICE

Their name refers to the fact that they hibernate. Only one species of dormouse is native to England, but on the continent, three species are found in northern Europe and one of these, the Edible or Fat Dormouse, has been introduced into England.

Hazel Dormouse
Muscardinus avellanarius

Identification
One of the prettiest rodents, it was once popular as a pet, which together with the reduction in coppiced woodland and hedgerows may account for its relative rarity today. It is a rich orange colour and has a furred tail and large eyes. It is most likely to be confused with the Wood Mouse, but that species does not have a furry tail. It grows to about 15 cm (6 in) of which the tail is less than half.

In the Garden
The Hazel Dormouse is only likely to be encountered in rural areas and each pair needs a relatively large area of woodland in which to forage, as they live at considerably lower densities than most other similar-sized rodents. There are several conservation programmes in operation to try to encourage this species. Although an agile climber, it is not particularly fast-moving, but as it is strictly nocturnal it is rarely seen. It nests in the base of coppice stools and hibernates among tree roots or in burrows; it can be encouraged to use artificial nest boxes.

Breeding
Dormice have 1 or 2 litters of up to 5 young, which are born naked and blind. The nest is in a cavity. They can live for up to 5 years.

Feeding
They feed on a wide variety of insect and vegetable matter, but are particularly noted for eating hazelnuts, which come into season prior to their going into hibernation.

Above: *Dormice hibernate, often using bird boxes. During hibernation, their temperature drops and they become completely torpid, relying on their fat reserves for the winter months. If you find one in a nest box, do not wake it.*

Left: *The Dormouse is easily recognized, as it is the only mouse that has a thickly furred tail. They are very agile and arboreal, but often make their nests near the ground.*

Edible Dormouse *Glis glis*

Identification
Edible Dormice look rather like miniature squirrels, being grey with a well furred tail. They have a total length of up to 35 cm (14 in), of which the tail is over half. They are almost exclusively nocturnal.

In the Garden
In Europe they are more widespread, occurring from the Pyrenees eastwards. They were introduced into England in 1902 by Lord Rothschild on his estate near Tring, Hertfordshire and, although they are not uncommon in the vicinity, they have never spread very far. However, Edible Dormice are common enough to be a minor pest, making a considerable amount of noise when they get into lofts and attics.

Above: *The characteristic 'robber's mask' face pattern of the Edible Dormouse might be confused with the similarly sized Flying Squirrel, but their ranges do not overlap.*

Below: *The Edible Dormouse eats large quantities of autumn fruits, which make it very fat – its other name is Fat Dormouse, because the Romans fattened the species as a table delicacy.*

Breeding
They have a single litter of up to 7 young, born blind and naked. The nest is in a cavity, such as an old woodpecker nest, or a nest box. These dormice are long-lived and can survive for up to 9 years.

Feeding
They feed on a wide range of fruit, nuts, berries and other plant matter and also insects, grubs and other invertebrates. The Romans kept dormice to fatten for the table. Like most hibernating mammals, they accumulate fat prior to going into hibernation and it was at this stage that these animals were prized for culinary purposes.

SQUIRRELS

Squirrels are medium-sized rodents, with prominent ears and bushy tails. Although most species are diurnal, a few are nocturnal. They feed mostly on fruit, seeds and vegetable matter, but also small animals. Squirrels store food, but often forget where they have stored it, and are consequently important dispersers of tree seeds.

Red Squirrel *Sciurus vulgaris*

Identification
Up to 25 cm (10 in) long plus a bushy tail of 20 cm (8 in). It is generally reddish or orange-brown above, white below, and has prominent ear tufts. In autumn and winter, the fur gradually bleaches, and the tail is often whitish.

In the Garden
Formerly widespread over much of Europe, and often occurring in parks and gardens, in most of the British Isles it is now extinct. Where it survives, it is mostly confined to places with large areas of coniferous forest. In other areas it has been displaced by the Grey Squirrel. Apart from a few isolated populations, the Red Squirrel is only really common in Scotland.

Breeding
Builds a nest or drey often in a tree fork, but also in old woodpeckers' holes, and crows' nests. It generally has 2 litters a year of up to 7 young.

Feeding
The Red Squirrel feeds mostly on pine kernels, seeds, nuts, and other vegetable matter, but also small animals, birds' eggs and nestlings, in season. Can be attracted to feeders with a variety of nuts and seeds.

Above: *Squirrels are extremely agile, and often take over bird feeders – whole books have been written about making feeders squirrel-proof.*

Below: *Red Squirrels occur in a wide variety of wooded habitats, but in Britain, where the Grey Squirrel has been introduced, they are now largely confined to coniferous forests.*

Grey Squirrel *Sciurus carolinensis*

Identification
Up to 30 cm (12 in) plus a tail of up to 24 cm (9.5 in). Generally grey, but often has an orange-brown tinge down the centre of the back. Never has ear tufts.

In the Garden
A native of North America, the Grey Squirrel was introduced into England at the end of the 19th century, and has since spread over much of the British Isles, usually displacing the native Red Squirrel. It is particularly abundant in suburban and parkland habitats, and a frequent visitor to bird feeders. In fact it is so successful, that many people feeding birds become obsessed with keeping squirrels away from their feeders.

Breeding
Like the Red Squirrel, the Grey Squirrel makes a drey in tree forks, old birds' nests and holes. It also enters lofts and attics to make its nests. It has 2 litters a year of up to 7 young, born blind, naked and helpless.

Feeding
Feeds on a wide range of vegetable matter, including tree shoots, leaves, berries, nuts and seeds, and also insects and small animals. It is easily attracted to feeders, taking peanuts, sunflower seed, coconut and many other foods. In areas where Red and Grey Squirrels occur together, weight sensitive feeders can be used to feed Red Squirrels, and exclude the Greys. A range of bird feeders that exclude Grey Squirrels is also available.

Flying Squirrel *Pteromys volans*

Identification
Smaller than other squirrels, and almost exclusively nocturnal. It has a length of up to 20 cm (8 in), and a tail of 14 cm (6 in), and webs of skin stretching between the fore and hind legs. It uses this to parachute and glide between trees.

In the Garden
Confined to north-eastern Europe and not found in the UK, the Flying Squirrel's range has been declining in recent years, due to forest clearance. It roosts and breeds in old woodpecker holes, and other cavities in old trees. It also readily adapts to nest boxes.

Above: *The Grey Squirrel is slightly larger than the Red, and is more adaptable. It is now common on feeders in suburban gardens in most parts of Britain.*

Below: *The Flying Squirrel is found right across northern Asia and in North America. In north-east Europe it is sometimes found in nest boxes, as well as old woodpecker holes.*

Breeding
Nests in holes, and has 2 litters a year of up to 4 young, born naked and helpless.

Feeding
It feeds on nuts, berries, seeds, as well as insects. During the winter it feeds on food stored in its nest.

FOX AND BADGER

The Fox and Badger are among the largest mammals commonly encountered in gardens. While Foxes are now remarkably common in many towns and cities, Badgers are generally confined to outer suburban areas, close to open countryside. Both are omnivorous and have learned to adapt to feeding on refuse and carrion. But because of this habit, they are also not infrequent roadkills themselves. Perhaps more surprising are recent reports of Otters moving into suburban areas – in the future, with more tolerant attitudes, they may become a frequent sight in gardens bordering canals and rivers.

Fox *Vulpes vulpes*

Identification
Dog-like, up to 90 cm (35 in) long, plus a tail of up to 60 cm (24 in). Generally a rusty reddish brown, with black on the back of the prominent ears, and a white tip to the bushy tail. The cubs are greyer, with less bushy tails.

In the Garden
Less than 50 years ago, Foxes were almost unknown outside rural areas, but in the 1960s they began to be observed in suburban and urban areas of Britain and northern Europe with increasing frequency. The main reason was the changing public attitude – previously Foxes were subject to intense persecution, both for their fur, and simply because predators were considered vermin. They are very agile, and easily climb fences and walls. Generally nocturnal, but when they are not disturbed will often come above ground during the day – particularly to bask in the sun. They often use railway embankments as corridors to move into the towns, and these are also favourite locations for their dens. Commuters often see families of young cubs playing in the morning sun in early spring. They often come into gardens backing onto railways.

Breeding
They breed underground in earths (dens) often under garden sheds, or in bramble patches. They have 4–6 cubs (occasionally more), and the entrance to the earth becomes very untidy with the remains of food.

Feeding
They scavenge roadkills, feed on mice, voles, and they also eat fruit such as blackberries. They can be fed with remains of poultry and other household scraps, or tinned catfood.

Below: *A vixen and her cub. These days the fox population in our gardens, especially older, bigger and quieter ones, is very healthy, mainly due to the wide availability of food.*

Badger *Meles meles*

Identification

A large, relatively nocturnal mammal easily recognized by its grey fur, distinctive black and white head markings, and a distinct bouncing gait. The head and body is up to 87 cm (34 in) long, with only a short tail, which is less than 20 cm (8 in).

In the Garden

Only likely to be encountered in gardens close to rural areas, or large parklands known to have badger setts (dens). Typical badger habitat is woodland close to open pasture or meadow. Badgers feed extensively on earthworms, and also need access to water. Except in particularly large gardens, they are very unlikely to breed, and they can cause considerable damage with their digging. In addition to digging for food they also dig 'latrine' pits some distance from their setts. However, the majority of people would probably tolerate damage for the enjoyment of seeing Badgers. Artificial setts can be built, but Badgers generally occupy traditional locations, some of which have been used for several centuries. They can be habituated to artificial light, in order to observe them – red light is less disturbing – but they will also become accustomed to ordinary household floodlights. They are often killed on roads, and in places where this is a regular occurrence, tunnels are very effective in reducing mortality.

Above: *Badgers are cautious, shy and relatively secretive animals, and are most likely to be glimpsed at night, when they are out foraging for food.*

Below: *Badgers generally prefer gardens, which have areas of lawn or grassland that supply them with their primary food source – earthworms – and covered areas in which to build their setts. For these reasons, larger gardens are preferred.*

Breeding

They have a single litter of up to 5 cubs, born underground, in early spring. The breeding setts are often very extensive, with numerous entrances, and they change the bedding regularly.

Feeding

Earthworms form a large proportion of the diet, but they also eat any small animals they find, including young mice and Rabbits. They can be fed with household scraps, as well as catfood, raw minced meat, eggs and milk. Peanut butter is among the more unusual foods used to attract badgers (and many rodents).

WEASELS AND MARTENS

Close relatives of the Badger and Otter, the Weasel, Stoat and martens are all predators. The Weasel is one of the smallest carnivores in the world, and the Stoat could be described as truly bloodthirsty. The martens are more omnivorous. Like many other carnivores, they have dense fur, which is often used in the garment industry. Large Weasels are sometimes longer than small Stoats, so size is not always a reliable way of identifying them. Most children know that they are 'weasily identified, because they are stoatally different'.

Above: *One of the world's tiniest carnivores, the Weasel is small enough to follow mice in their tunnels and burrows. It is most often seen dashing across a road.*

Weasel *Mustela nivalis*

Identification
Tiny, with a head and body of 11–25 cm (4.5–10 in) and a tail of about 9 cm (3.5 in), it is a rich reddish brown above and white below. The tail does not have a black tip. In the north of its range it turns white in winter.

In the Garden
Uncommon in gardens, and normally only encountered in fairly rural areas or on the edge of cities and towns. If they are seen, they can be attracted by 'squeaking'. They can be encouraged by using sheets of corrugated iron, but their presence will be dependent on the numbers of mice and voles – their principal prey.

Breeding
Weasels nest in underground burrows, and have 2 litters a year of up to 12 young, but usually fewer than 6, which are born naked and helpless.

Feeding
Almost exclusively carnivorous, Weasels feed on mice and voles, which they hunt in their burrows.

Stoat *Mustela erminea*

Identification
Larger than the very similar Weasel, growing to a total length of over 30 cm (12 in), of which the tail is about half. The fur is a rich reddish brown above, yellowish white below, and the tail tip is black. In winter, the more northerly populations turn white, except for the tail tip which remains black. This is the ermine fur that is used on regalia.

In the Garden
Like the Weasel it is a relatively uncommon visitor to

Below: *The Stoat, although small, is usually significantly larger than the Weasel, and feeds on larger prey – up to the size of Rabbits and domestic fowl.*

gardens, but where Rabbits are common, they may be a more frequent visitor. Stoats can easily be attracted by squeaking, which is the high-pitched 'kissing' sound made with the lips on the back of the hand.

Breeding
Generally has one litter a year of up to 12 young, born blind and helpless.

Feeding
Although Stoats are carnivores, they feed extensively on the blood of their prey. They often attack Rabbits and poultry considerably larger than themselves, biting the jugular vein, which means the victim quickly becomes unconscious, and they lap up the blood.

Above: *In the northern parts of their range Stoats usually turn white in winter – except for the black tip to the tail. In the south this occurs only occasionally.*

Right: *The Pine Marten, once on the verge of extinction in the British Isles, is slowly recovering, and in some parts of Scotland is a regular visitor to feeding tables. But its spread is slow, and it has been suggested that reintroductions into its former range might help.*

Pine Marten *Martes martes*

Identification
A large relative of the Weasel, the Pine Marten grows to a length of over 50 cm (20 in), with a bushy tail of about 25 cm (10 in). It is a rich, dark brown above, with a yellowish-white throat and belly. It is very agile and largely arboreal.

In the Garden
Its range is very much reduced, having been persecuted both for its fur and because it preys on birds. In the British Isles it is likely to be encountered only in the Highlands of Scotland and in Ireland. However, in those areas where it is no longer persecuted, it can become relatively tame and a regular visitor to feeders. In continental Europe the closely related Beech Marten is more commonly found in suburban areas, often nesting in attics and outhouses.

Breeding
It makes its nest in tree holes, disused birds' nests, and in rock crevices. A single litter of up to 7 (usually fewer) young is born in summer. At birth, the blind and helpless young are covered in pale fur.

Feeding
Mostly carnivorous, feeding on birds, squirrels, and other animals, but also taking fruit in season. Pine Martens can be attracted to feeders using household scraps, fat, minced meat, and the like.

RABBIT AND HARES

Rabbits and hares are superficially similar to rodents, but not particularly closely related. They have enlarged incisors like rodents, but also have a small second set behind the incisors. They are relatively large, active by day and night and, although they can occur in larger gardens, there is always potential conflict with horticulture. The Mountain or Varying Hare occurs in the Highlands of Scotland, Ireland and a few upland areas of England and Wales. Neither the Rabbit nor the Brown Hare is native to Britain. Hares are believed to have been introduced in the Iron Age or soon after and Rabbits during the early Middle Ages. Rabbits were originally confined to enclosed warrens, where they were bred for meat and fur. In recent years both species have declined. The Rabbit was almost exterminated during the 1950s by the introduction of myxomatosis, but recovered and now has considerable immunity. The Brown Hare is declining, largely due to modern intensive farming practices.

Rabbit *Oryctolagus cuniculus*

Identification
Up to 55 cm (22 in) long, plus a fluffy tail of up to 7 cm (2.8 in). The general fur colour is greyish brown and the ears are long. This is the wild ancestor of the Domestic Rabbit and some populations often have a proportion of black individuals. Rabbits usually live in warrens (a complex of burrows) which they excavate in

Below: *Rabbits on the edge of a colony stand on their hind legs to keep watch for predators. When they are alarmed, they thump the ground with their hind feet to warn the rest of the colony.*

Above: *Rabbits are born naked and helpless in a nest underground. The mother leaves the young during the day, blocking the nest burrow to protect them. They stay close to the burrow until they are independent of the mother.*

embankments and they generally deposit their droppings in heaps.

In the Garden
Most gardeners try to keep Rabbits out of their garden, since they can cause enormous damage in a very short space of time. However, in a large garden, they can be part of a balanced ecosystem. In a small garden, exclusion, using rabbit fencing, is normally the best solution and is relatively simple and cheap. In a large garden, an embankment with a warren would make an attractive addition.

Breeding
The ability of Rabbits to breed rapidly is well known: they produce up to 5 litters a year. They make a nest in an underground burrow (occasionally above ground in a bramble patch or thick cover) and give birth to 3–8 young, which are born blind and naked. The young

emerge from their burrows at about 3 weeks and are sexually mature at around 5 months.

Feeding
They feed mostly on grass and other herbage, but in hard weather, when snow covers the ground, they eat tree bark. They graze close to the ground, and can cause considerable damage to plants in a garden.

Brown Hare *Lepus europaeus*

Identification
About 70 cm (28 in) long, with a short fluffy tail, white below, dark above. The ears are long, and black-tipped. Brown Hares are significantly larger than Rabbits. When disturbed they will often run into open country, whereas Rabbits invariably dive for cover. Hares have very prominent eyes on the side of the head, giving them almost 360° vision.

In the Garden
Hares are likely to be encountered in gardens only in rural areas. Although most often seen in open fields, they are also found in woodland as well, especially in winter. Because they have very large home ranges, it is difficult to persuade hares to take up permanent residence in a garden.

Breeding
Brown Hares give birth to well developed young, usually 2–4, which are born fully furred. For the first few days the young stay close together, but gradually disperse, coming to the mother at dawn and dusk to feed. They breed in almost all months of the year and have up to 4 litters a year.

Feeding
Exclusively vegetarian, eating a wide range of plants, including grasses and crops. They often 'garden'; this means they bite off all the young branches of newly planted trees and shrubs. Although most gardeners probably will not wish to attract them, they can be fed by leaving prunings from willow and other trees.

Above: *Brown Hares are relatively large, with characteristic long, black-tipped ears. Their eyes are at the side of the head, enabling them to see behind them.*

Right: *Brown Hares do not live in burrows or make nests, instead, they make a shallow 'form', often in a furrow in a ploughed field, or in the shelter of a tussock.*

DEER

Deer are not animals usually associated with gardens, but they occur with surprising frequency in many parts of Britain, and not just in rural areas. They are generally secretive and nocturnal, and may go unnoticed but for their distinctive tracks. Of the six species found in the British Isles, only two are native, and even these have been moved around over the years. Siberian Roe Deer have been introduced and may have hybridized with the native species, and the American Wapiti may have hybridized with Red Deer, which also hyrbidizes with Sika.

Above: *The Muntjac Deer has short spiky antlers, and a bony ridge, giving it a characteristic face pattern.*

Muntjac *Muntiacus reevesi*

Identification
The size of a medium-sized dog, the Muntjac grows to about 90 cm (35 in), with a shoulder height of about 50 cm (20 in). It is a reddish brown and has a brush-like tail which is white on the underside, and often flashed as it runs away. The male's antlers are short and spiky. They are generally solitary, or in small family groups, but never in herds.

In the Garden
Originally from Asia, Muntjacs escaped into the wild around Woburn and Whipsnade in Bedfordshire, and have since spread widely in central and southern England. Although generally nocturnal, if they are left undisturbed, they will eventually become fairly tame. They can cause extensive damage, and are often described as being particularly partial to roses.

Breeding
A single fawn is born, almost any time of the year, at around 7 month intervals. It is active shortly after birth.

Feeding
Muntjacs browse on leaves of a wide range of plants, and also eat grass and tree bark.

Roe Deer *Capreolus capreolus*

Identification
A native species, the Roe Deer looks rather similar to the Muntjac, but stands about 70 cm (27 in) high at the shoulders and has a more upright stance. The male's antlers are longer than the Muntjac's, with more branching.

In the Garden
Although mostly found in woodlands, it occasionally comes into gardens in rural areas, but being nocturnal and shy it is very rarely seen.

Breeding
Two sometimes 3 spotted fawns are born in spring.

Feeding
Like most other deer Roe Deer are mainly browsers, and can do considerable damage to trees in winter.

Below: *The Roe Deer is native to the British Isles, but only likely to be seen in larger gardens and parkland. When rubbing the 'velvet' off their antlers they can damage trees.*

Chinese Water Deer
Hypropotes inermis

Identification
A small deer, usually seen singly, in pairs or family groups, it was introduced into Britain in the 1940s and has since spread over a wide area of southern England. Unlike most other deer neither sex has antlers, but the male has long tusks. It stands about 50 cm (20 in) high at the shoulder.

In the Garden
As its name suggests it is often found in swampy habitats, and in East Anglia it is a regular visitor to gardens in and around nature reserves and other areas where it occurs.

Breeding
Prolific, with up to 6 fawns (usually 2–4), but suffers heavy mortality in hard winters.

Feeding
As with the other deer, it browses and grazes.

Below: *This deer is another exotic species that has become well established in the wild. Unusually, this species has tusks.*

Above: *The male Fallow Deer has palmate antlers. This species is common in parklands and the gardens of stately homes, where it is often kept in a semi-domesticated state.*

Fallow Deer *Cervus dama*

Identification
A parkland deer, the Fallow Deer is particularly attractive, and often dappled with a Bambi-like pattern on the back. White individuals also occur as well as uniformly dark ones. The male or buck has flattened 'palmate' antlers and stands almost 1 m (36–38 in) at the shoulders.

In the Garden
Fallow Deer are often kept in parks around stately homes, where they live in herds. Escapees are found in many parts of England and small herds persist in local woodlands. They may occasionally wander into larger gardens.

Breeding
Mating occurs during autumn. Fawns are born in May or June, usually only one but sometimes 2 or even 3.

Feeding
Fallow Deer feed largely on the young shoots and bark of trees, but also depend on acorns, chestnuts and horse-chestnuts. They also graze and browse on lawns and grasses.

WATERBIRDS

Most waterbirds need fairly large bodies of water to take up residence, and they may not be welcome in a small garden with a small pond, because of the damage they can do. However, a wide range of waterbirds can occur in larger gardens that have big ponds or lakes. Many gardeners will also introduce collections of native or exotic waterfowl if they have sufficient space. Larger gardens may attract Canada Geese, Mute Swans, Mandarin Ducks, Tufted Ducks, Shoveler and many other species.

Mallard *Anas platyrhynchos*

Identification
The male is 51–62 cm (20–24 in) in length, with a glossy dark green head and neck, and a thin white ring around the neck separating the green from a purple-brown breast. The underside is grey and it has a dark purple-blue wing patch (speculum), edged with white. The male has distinctive curly feathers on the rump. The female is much duller, with a generally brown plumage, very similar to the plumage of many other species of duck.

In the Garden
In larger gardens with ponds and lakes, Mallards are common, and even in relatively small gardens they will sometimes take up residence.

Breeding
Mallards start nesting in early spring and continue until late summer. They may have more than one brood if they lose their ducklings to predators. They lay up to 12 large duck-egg blue eggs, which hatch after 4 weeks.

Feeding
A surface feeder, commonly 'dabbling', and also upending to feed on waterweeds and aquatic invertebrates. In the garden they will take grain or pellets.

Below: *Mallard often nest in larger gardens, or can be seen around suburban parks in spring.*

Above: *Moorhens are common in most parks and larger gardens with ponds. The chicks have jet-black down and bob on the water's surface.*

Moorhen *Gallinula chloropus*

Identification
A medium-sized waterbird of up to 33 cm (13 in), and mostly black. It has a bright orange-red bill and shield to the front of the head, and white on the wings and undertail. The legs and feet are greenish yellow, with lobes of skin on the toes. They swim with a characteristic jerking movement. The Coot is rather similar, but has a white forehead, and is generally found on larger bodies of water.

In the Garden
Widespread and familiar in many types of wetlands, but generally not on larger more open waters. Often occurs in gardens with larger ponds, particularly if there is vegetation around the margins such as rushes and flags.

Breeding
Builds a large, often floating, nest at the water's edge, and lays 5–11 eggs, which are greyish, greenish or buff with speckling and blotches. The eggs hatch after 19–22 days, and the young can fly at about 6–7 weeks old.

Feeding
Omnivorous, it will become very tame in gardens, feeding on grain, poultry pellets, and the like.

Dabchick *Tachybaptus ruficollis*

Identification
A very small, 25 cm (10 in), dumpy waterbird, that appears dark brown. At close range chestnut-brown cheeks can be seen, with a white spot at the base of the bill.

In the Garden
Only ever likely to occur in a garden with at least a small lake or very large pond. Since they have difficulty taking off and landing, they need a long clear run and no over hanging vegetation or steep banks. However, they do prefer ponds with rushes and other marginals. They dive frequently, reappearing some distance away each time they surface.

Breeding
The Dabchick nests at the water's edge, building with water weeds and other vegetation. It lays 4–6 eggs, which are white, but become stained during incubation. The eggs hatch after 19–25 days and the young fly at about 6–8 weeks.

Feeding
Feeds exclusively on aquatic life, including small fish and invertebrates.

Above: A rarity in all but the very largest gardens, Dabchicks are often seen in parks. The young are striped, and like the parents are first-class divers.

Below: Although mostly found on rivers and larger lakes, in winter Kingfishers often wander and may turn up on a garden pond for a day or two.

Kingfisher *Alcedo atthis*

Identification
The Kingfisher is unmistakable with a brilliant blue above, an orange underside and a long red bill. Its total length is about 16 cm (6 in).

In the Garden
Not likely to be resident in most gardens, except those bordering rivers and streams. In autumn young birds often wander and may turn up in gardens for a few days, if there is a pond well stocked with small fish.

Breeding
Kingfishers excavate nest tunnels up to 1 m (39 in) long in sandy banks and lay 6–7 round, white eggs on a nest of bones and food remains. The eggs hatch after 19–21 days and the young fledge in 3–4 weeks.

Feeding
It eats small fish and insects.

WADING BIRDS AND GAMEBIRDS

Wading birds are certainly not the sort of birds one would expect in the average garden. However, even in urban areas herons are surprisingly common – as many fish keepers have learned to their cost. Many smaller waders occur with surprising regularity in parks, on river banks, and reservoirs, and are heard flying over towns and cities while on migration. Pheasants are often surprisingly common in rural gardens.

Grey Heron *Ardea cinerea*

Identification
A large, long-legged, long-necked grey bird, with a total length of nearly a metre (39 in). Mostly shades of grey, with a black crest. In flight the head is held back, with the neck in an 'S' shape, and the wingbeats are very slow.

In the Garden
Only likely to occur if there is a pond, particularly if there are Goldfish. Unless it is a very large garden, with a significant population of fish, Herons are most likely to be only sporadic visitors.

Breeding
They breed in colonies, usually in tops of very tall trees. They build large stick nests, which are repaired and used year after year. They lay 3–5 greenish-blue eggs, which hatch after 23–28 days, and the young leave the nest at about 50–55 days.

Feeding
They feed on fish, amphibians, and any other animals they can catch, including young birds. They can be kept away from garden ponds relatively easily (see page 58).

Below: *Grey Herons are found in the centre of many towns and cities now that they are no longer persecuted. They often visit garden ponds and steal Goldfish and other fish.*

Above: *Once a common sight in towns and villages all over Europe, White Storks are now comparatively rare. They can be attracted by using nesting poles – traditionally with a cart wheel.*

White Stork *Ciconia alba*

Identification
Very large at up to 1.15 m (45 in) in length, White Storks are white with black flight feathers on the wings, and a long, bright red bill and long, bright red legs.

In the Garden
Once a familiar sight over most of Europe, breeding in towns and cities as well as rural areas, it has long been extinct in Britain, and is increasingly rare over most of Europe.

Breeding
White Storks build huge nests on roof tops, chimneys and treetops, and can be encouraged with artificial platforms, traditionally in the form of old cartwheels. The nests are used for many years, and they lay up to 5 white eggs, which hatch after 4–5 weeks. The young fledge at 8–9 weeks.

Feeding
A wide variety of small animals, including amphibians, fish, rodents, as well as grasshoppers and other large insects.

Common Sandpiper
Actitis hypoleucos

Identification
A small wader, seen in a wide range of wetland habitats on migration, including river banks, and reservoirs. It is about 20 cm (8 in) long, brown above, white below, and has a characteristic, constant, bobbing motion.

In the Garden
Waders only rarely occur in gardens, but this may be because there is no suitable habitat for them. In rural areas, larger gardens with lakes and ponds could be made more attractive by creating expanses of shallow muddy edges; it is likely that this additional feature would bring in migrating waders, particularly sandpipers, but also Snipe and Lapwing, Redshank and others.

Breeding
Common Sandpipers breed over much of northern Europe, but in recent years their numbers have declined. In Britain they are now mostly confined to upland areas.

Feeding
Common Sandpipers feed on small invertebrates found at the water's edge.

Above: *Any really large pond or small lake could attract waders such as this Common Sandpiper. This species also occasionally pauses during migration on rivers and streams in built-up areas.*

In the Garden
In rural areas they frequently enter gardens, where they can cause extensive damage to plants. They are not native to northern Europe, and in many areas their numbers are maintained by release of farm-bred birds.

Breeding
They nest under bushes and in thick cover, on the ground, laying up to 15 relatively large eggs, which are pale olive. They do not start incubating until the clutch is complete, so that all hatch simultaneously after 3–4 weeks.

Feeding
They feed on invertebrates during the breeding season. They also eat grain and weed seeds, as well as shoots of crops and other plants.

Pheasant
Phasianus colchicus

Identification
A large, long-tailed gamebird, of up to 90 cm (35 in). The male has iridescent bronze plumage, a bright red face, dark green neck and usually a white neck ring. The female has a shorter tail, and is duller with a closely barred, brown plumage giving her excellent camouflage when incubating her eggs.

Left: *Common Pheasants are spectacularly plumaged, but in a small garden they can be a pest, since they dig and scratch, and will spoil flower- and seed-beds.*

BIRDS OF PREY

Hawks suffered massive population declines in the 19th century, as a result of persecution by gamekeepers, and then in the 1950s they suffered further declines owing to the effects of persistent pesticides. By the end of the 20th century the numbers of several species were beginning to recover, and some were also being helped by conservation programmes. The Peregrine Falcon has recently started colonizing some towns in Britain.

Above: *Kestrels are a familiar site hovering over motorway verges, and they breed in and around most cities and towns, often nesting on buildings such as tower blocks.*

Kestrel *Falco tinnunculus*

Identification
Up to 36 cm (14 in), the male has a grey head, brown back with black spotting and dark grey wings and tail; the underside is pale buff with dark streaks. The female is generally browner and more barred. Kestrels have long pointed wings, and are frequently seen hovering. The call is a high-pitched rapid, 'kee-kee-kee-kee'.

In the Garden
Kestrels are the commonest bird of prey, and are frequently seen hovering over roadsides, fields, and waste ground. They occasionally hunt in gardens, and can be spotted overhead practically anywhere. They are often seen perched on telegraph poles and fences alongside busy motorways.

Breeding
Kestrels nest in tree holes, on high buildings and adapt to nest boxes readily. They nest from March to July and lay 3–6 pale buff eggs, blotched with brown. The eggs hatch after about 4 weeks, and the young fledge 4–5 weeks later.

Feeding
They feed mostly on voles, mice and large insects caught on the ground. They also take birds, frogs and almost any other small animal.

Red Kite *Milvus milvus*

Identification
A large bird of prey, up to 65 cm (26 in) in length, it is reddish brown with a wingspan of up to 1.9 m (74 in) and a deeply forked tail. Red Kites are usually seen soaring overhead, but are capable of remarkable agility as they snatch prey from the ground or a bird table. The Common Buzzard can also be seen flying overhead in many gardens within its range; it has rounded wings, and does not have a forked tail.

In the Garden
A quarter of a century ago the Red Kite was one of the rarest birds breeding in Britain. Then the Welsh population began to recover, and introductions back into England also succeeded.

Right: *Once a familiar sight all over Europe, the Red Kite vanished from most of Britain, but is making a comeback. It will take food scraps from garden bird tables.*

Its recovery has continued, and now it is a common sight in many parts of the country and an increasingly regular visitor to gardens, particularly where food is put out for it.

Breeding

They nest in tall trees 6–33 m (20–100 ft) high, often taking over an old crow's nest or building a large twig nest. They lay 2 or 3 eggs, which are whitish with brown spotting. The eggs hatch after about one month, and the young fledge 45–50 days later, and are fed by the parents for a further 3 weeks.

Feeding

Red Kites prey on almost anything they can catch, but are also scavengers taking carrion such as road kills. They can be attracted to gardens in areas where they occur by putting out remains of poultry and other carrion.

Sparrowhawk *Accipiter nisus*

Identification

A round-winged, fast-flying hawk that often appears in a garden, then disappears, seeming to fly straight through bushes and trees. When perched, its closely barred underside is clearly visible. Up to 38 cm (15 in) in length the females are larger than the males. In the open, the Sparrowhawk usually flies very close to the ground.

Above: *After a serious decline in the second half of the 20th century, Sparrowhawks are once again a familiar sight in gardens, often breeding in taller trees.*

Below: *Sparrowhawks feed mostly on small birds, and can become very unpopular as they soon realise that bird tables attract a ready supply of their prey.*

In the Garden

Although once confined to rural areas, it is now common in many suburban areas of the British Isles.

Breeding

The Sparrowhawk builds a nest in a tree or bush, sometimes utilizing an old crow's nest, in late spring or summer. It lays 3–6 eggs, which are pale blue with brown blotches. The eggs hatch after an incubation of 4–5 weeks and the young fledge 3–4 weeks later.

Feeding

Mostly small birds, up to the size of Wood Pigeons. Sparrowhawks capture their prey in flight, and carry it to a feeding post to pluck it, if the prey is too large, then they feed on the ground.

DOVES AND PIGEONS

The names dove and pigeon are to a large extent interchangeable. They are relatively large birds, often gregarious and some species are migratory. The Rock Dove has been domesticated for many centuries, and the knowledge gained from the discussions with breeders of fancy varieties of pigeons was instrumental in allowing Charles Darwin to understand the section process in evolution.

Above: *Before the middle of the 20th century, Wood Pigeons were rare in towns and suburbs, but they are now one of the most familiar garden birds.*

Below: *The Feral Pigeon, often known as the 'London' Pigeon, was originally a cliff-dwelling species, which readily adapted to the urban environment.*

Wood Pigeon *Columba palumbus*

Identification
A large pigeon of up to 40 cm (16 in) that at first glance appears grey, with white, but actually has some very beautiful and subtle colouring. The adult has a white mark on each side of the neck, giving it its alternative name of Ring Dove, and they have a white edge to the wing, which becomes very obvious in flight. The call is a loud, repetitive, 'coo-COO-coo coo-coo'.

In the Garden
Very common, feeding on lawns, and nesting in tall hedges and trees.

Breeding
Builds a flimsy nest of twigs and usually lays two pure white eggs, which hatch after 16–17 days. The young fledge at about 3–5 weeks.

Feeding
Feeds mostly on plant matter, and can strip brassicas (the cabbage family) in an allotment, and cause considerable damage to a wide range of seedlings. It also takes grain, feeding on bird tables or on the spilled food beneath.

Feral Pigeon *Columba livia*

Identification
The feral descendant of the Domestic Pigeon, and up to 34 cm (13 in), it comes in an infinite variety of colours and patterns, but is too familiar to need detailed description. It is very similar to the much more elusive Stock Dove, which can occur in larger gardens in rural areas.

In the Garden
Often common, particularly in more urban areas. Its original habitat was cliff and sea caves, and the urban landscape of high-rise buildings provides an adequate replacement, provided food is available. In the past many town centres had huge populations, but modern concerns over public health have led to bans on pigeon feeding, and a consequent reduction in numbers. Peregrine Falcons often prey on Feral Pigeons.

Breeding

Feral Pigeons nest on ledges, making very little effort at nest building, and lay 2 pure white eggs, which hatch after 16–19 days, and the young fledge at about 4–5 weeks. When food is available, they nest almost all the year round, and the young start breeding when about 6 months old.

Feeding

Almost omnivorous, relying on household scraps and waste, but preferring grain and seeds.

Turtle Dove *Streptopelia turtur*

Identification

A rather delicate, small dove, 26–28 cm (10–11 in) in length, with very intricate and attractive markings. The wings have a scaly appearance, and on the neck there is an obvious black and white collar. Most of the body colour is pinkish. The song is a very distinctive, rhythmic monotonous churring.

In the Garden

A summer visitor, arriving in southern Britain and northern Europe in late April or May. It is common only in larger gardens in rural areas. In recent years it has declined, and part of the reason is that it is extensively hunted in many parts of southern Europe.

Breeding

Nests in hedges, bushes and trees, building a stick nest and laying one or two white eggs. The eggs hatch after 13–14 days, and the young fledge about 3 weeks later. Normally 2 broods are raised, occasionally a third.

Feeding

The Turtle Dove feeds mostly on seeds, usually of plants which are defined as weeds.

Collared Dove *Streptopelia decaocto*

Identification

Up to 32 cm (13 in) in length, it is overall pinkish grey with a white-edged black collar, and black wing tips. The voice is a monotonous, tri-syllabic 'coooo-COOOO-cooo'.

In the Garden

A recent colonist of western Europe, it first arrived in Britain in the 1950s, and has since become very common in suburban and rural areas. It is easily attracted to feeders.

Above: *The Turtle Dove is a summer migrant which arrives in Britain in late spring, having run the gauntlet of southern European hunters.*

Breeding

The Collared Dove breeds almost all the year round, producing up to 5 broods a year. The nest is a flimsy stick affair, and 2 white eggs are laid, which hatch after 14–18 days, and the young fledge 2–3 weeks later.

Feeding

They feed mostly on grain.

Below: *The Collared Dove was unknown in Europe prior to World War II. Its spread from Asia Minor was rapid, reaching Britain in the 1950s and now it is found even as far north as the Hebrides off Scotland.*

OWLS

Owls are nocturnal birds of prey. However, several species do hunt in daylight, particularly in winter when the day length is short. Owls all have binocular vision and acute hearing – some species, such as the Tawny, use their hearing when hunting. Some species are subject to wide population fluctuations owing to food availability. Most, but not all, nest in holes.

Tawny Owl *Strix aluco*

Identification
Also known as the Brown Owl, the Tawny Owl grows to 39 cm (15.5 in). The plumage is soft and very variable in colouring, but usually various shades of browns and greys. Its typical call is a 'too-wit too-woo', and it also has a sharp, high-pitched 'kee-wik' call.

In the Garden
Common and widespread, even in the centre of large towns and cities. Strictly nocturnal, it does not normally emerge to hunt until after sunset. However, if it is disturbed, and other birds find it during daylight, they will draw attention to the Tawny Owl by mobbing it.

Below: The Tawny Owl is normally strictly nocturnal, but sometimes can be seen by day, usually when other birds discover one roosting, and mob it, noisily drawing attention to it.

Breeding
Tawny Owls usually nest in holes, and sometimes adapt to nest boxes, particularly in areas where there is a shortage of natural tree holes. The nest is rudimentary and consists largely of feathers and food remains. They lay 2–5 pure white, round eggs, which are incubated for about a month, and the young fledge around 5 weeks later.

Feeding
They feed on a wide range of animals, including mice, insects, frogs and small birds.

Little Owl *Athene noctua*

Identification
Smaller than a Blackbird at 23 cm (9 in), it is rather short-tailed and has a plump silhouette. It is heavily spotted, and has yellow eyes and characteristic whitish 'eyebrows', which give it a frowning expression. It has a bouncing, undulating flight, and often perches on posts and also on the ground. It is rather vocal, and some of its calls are similar to the 'kee-wick' call of the Tawny Owl.

In the Garden
In rural areas it is relatively common and will occur in larger gardens. It is not native to Britain, but since its introduction from continental Europe in the 19th century, it has become widespread.

Breeding
It nests in old woodpecker holes as well as natural cavities, and adapts readily to nest boxes. It lays 3–5 white, spherical eggs, which are incubated for 4–5 weeks. The young fledge at about 4 weeks, but stay around the nest site and are fed by the parents for another 3 weeks.

Feeding
The Little Owl feeds mostly on insects and invertebrates, also small birds and mammals. It often feeds on roads in warm weather, on the insects attracted to the warmth.

Barn Owl *Tyto alba*

Identification
Up to 36 cm (14 in) in length, this white or very pale owl, looks very white in flight. At rest the characteristic heart-shaped face can be seen. In flight it often appears rather large-headed. It hunts in open areas, often hovering, and is often active by day, particularly after prolonged bad weather, and in winter. The call is a bloodcurdling screech.

In the Garden
Barn Owls are mostly found in rural areas, although they occasionally occur in parks and gardens in rural towns. They nest and roost in barns, church towers and other man-made structures as well as hollow trees. They are one of the most widely distributed birds in the world. Their numbers crashed in Britain in the latter part of the 20th century, but they are slowly recovering.

Breeding
Barn Owls nest in dark cavities, and readily adapt to nest boxes and other artificial sites, laying up to 7 white eggs at 2-day intervals. The eggs hatch at 2-day intervals, after an incubation of 4–5 weeks. When the adults are unable to catch sufficient food the older chicks sometimes devour the younger ones. They leave the nest after about 7 weeks, but are fed by the adults for several more weeks.

Feeding
The Barn Owl generally feeds on rodents, particularly rats and voles, but also a wide range of other prey.

Above: *The Little Owl is often seen in broad daylight, perched on a fence post, and has a characteristic bobbing motion. It also feeds on insects attracted to roads at dusk.*

Right: *Barn Owls are slowly returning to their former range in Britain, having declined dramatically in the second half of the 20th century.*

MARTINS, SWIFT AND SWALLOW

Swifts are not closely related to Swallows and martins despite their superficial similarity. All are adapted for fast flight, with long narrow wings and all are summer migrants, spending the winter months in Africa. Their numbers in Europe are influenced by conditions in Africa as much as they are on their breeding grounds.

Above: House Martins need a good supply of mud to build or repair their nests, so in towns where this might be difficult to find, providing artificial nests is often a help.

House Martin *Delichon urbica*

Identification
Blue-black above, contrasting with the brilliant white underside and with a characteristic white rump. It is about 12.5 cm (5 in) long and the tail is only slightly forked. The Sand Martin, which generally prefers more rural areas, but may occur, particularly on migration, is brown above, has a brown chest band and lacks the white rump.

In the Garden
House Martins are a common sight over gardens in almost all areas including the centre of towns. They may also nest if suitable sites are available. They are familiar summer visitors throughout most of Europe.

Breeding
House Martins build a mud nest under the eaves of houses, on water towers and other similar man-made structures. Although they once nested in caves and on cliffs, these sites are now very rarely used. The nest is lined with feathers and 3–5 whitish eggs incubated for

14–16 days. The young fledge after 2–3 weeks. There are usually 2 or 3 broods. Artificial nests should be emptied and cleaned during the winter in order to rid them of parasites.

Feeding
House Martins feed exclusively on insects and other invertebrates which they catch on the wing.

Swift *Apus apus*

Identification
A very fast-flying uniformly dark bird with scimitar-like wings and a forked tail, and up to 17 cm (6.5 in) long. Swifts often fly high, particularly at dusk, when they climb to roost on the wing. In late summer they often form screaming parties, chasing through towns and villages near their nesting sites.

Below: Swifts are among the most aerial of all birds, mating on the wing. Once they fledge, they fly to Africa and back without ever settling. They appear crescent shaped in flight.

Above: *Swifts nest under eaves – good substitutes for their natural nest sites of cave entrances and cliffs – often well into the centre of towns and cities. They can live to 15 years or more.*

In the Garden

Swifts are widespread in Europe, and although in parts of Scandinavia they still nest in tree holes, over most of their range they nest almost exclusively in man-made structures. They are one of the most aerial birds, only settling on their nests, spending the rest of the year entirely on the wing.

Breeding

They nest in colonies mostly under the eaves of houses, although they will also use specially designed bricks. The nest is an untidy one, made of scraps and feathers collected on the wing and they lay 2–3 white, rather round eggs, which hatch after an incubation of up to 27 days and the young fledge at up to 8 weeks.

Feeding

Swifts feed exclusively on the wing, taking large numbers of aphids and other small 'aerial plankton', which also includes spiders.

Swallow *Hirundo rustica*

Identification

Glossy blue above, whitish below, with a reddish chestnut throat and forehead. Its total length is up to 22 cm (8.5 in) and this includes its characteristic and distinctive long tail streamers. In flight the tail is deeply forked. The young lack the long tail streamers. Swallows are often seen perched on telegraph wires. They have a twittering song, either on the wing or from a perch.

In the Garden

Once a very familiar sight, their numbers have declined dramatically. This is mainly due to reduction in numbers of flying insects – until the early 20th century there were huge numbers of horses and cattle kept in and around towns and villages, providing breeding sites and associated insects, which were suitable for Swallows.

Breeding

Like House Martins, Swallows nest almost exclusively in man-made structures. In particular, they nest in barns, byres and other agricultural buildings and also garden sheds. The nest is usually in a dark recess, on a beam, and is built from grasses and other vegetation, lined with feathers. They lay 4–5 eggs, which are whitish with pinkish red spots, and hatch after about 14–16 days. The young fledge after about 3 weeks.

Feeding

Swallows feed exclusively on small flying insects and other invertebrates.

Below: *In autumn, Swallows gather in large evening roosts prior to migrating south to Africa. They often congregate on telephone wires and electricity cables.*

WOODPECKERS AND PARROTS

These include the most colourful birds seen in the garden. Woodpeckers are hole-nesters and will sometimes use nest boxes, but generally excavate their own nest holes. The one species of parakeet is not native to Europe, but feral populations are now well established and nest in old woodpecker holes and nest boxes.

Green Woodpecker
Picus viridis

Identification
Up to 33 cm (13 in), this relatively large bird is brilliant greenish yellow on the rump, which is clearly visible as it flies away, with characteristic undulating flight. The adults have bright red on the head and the back and wings are green. More often seen on the ground than other woodpeckers. Its call is a distinctive 'laugh' – a loud, 'hew-hew-hew' – giving it its older country name of Yaffle.

In the Garden
Regular visitors, particularly in autumn and winter, when they come to lawns to feed on ants. In the breeding season they are confined to areas with large trees.

Breeding
Nest in tree holes, laying 5–7 white eggs, which hatch after 18–19 days. The young fledge at about 18–21 days.

Feeding
They feed on wood-boring insects and their grubs and ants. They are relatively uncommon on feeders.

Great Spotted Woodpecker
Dendrocopus major

Identification
Smaller than the Green Woodpecker at up to 23 cm (9 in), it is mostly black and white, with a bright red patch under the tail and bright red on the back of the head in the male. The female lacks red on the head and the juveniles have it extending on the crown.

In the Garden
The Great Spotted is the most common and widespread woodpecker in the garden.

Above: *The Great Spotted Woodpecker is a common and spectacular visitor to garden bird feeders. It is particularly fond of peanuts.*

Left: *Green Woodpeckers are generally found only in larger gardens and parks. However, in winter they often visit gardens, and are seen feeding on lawns where they search for ants.*

Breeding

Excavates a nest hole usually above 3 m (10 ft) from the ground. Lays 4–7 glossy white eggs, which hatch after 16 days, and leave the nest at about 18–21 days.

Feeding

Mostly wood-boring grubs and other insects. Great Spotted Woodpeckers are frequent visitors to feeders, and are particularly fond of suet and peanuts.

Ring-necked Parakeet
Psittacula krameri

Identification

An unmistakable, bright green bird, with a long tail, with a total length of 40 cm (16 in) of which the tail is about half. The decurved bill is bright red and it has a narrow red and black ring around the neck. It makes a wide range of chattering and screeching calls, and is very noisy in flight.

In the Garden

This is a native of Asia. The populations in Britain are now well established and were the result of escapes and deliberate releases from about 1970 onwards. They are largely confined to suburban areas and are heavily dependent on being fed.

Breeding

Ring-necked Parakeets are hole nesters, using old woodpecker holes and nest boxes. They start nesting in January and lay one or two clutches of white, almost spherical eggs. The eggs are incubated for just over 3 weeks and the young leave the nest 6–7 weeks later.

Feeding

They feed on a wide range of plant matter, but prefer fruits and peanuts.

Above: *The amount of red on a Great Spotted Woodpecker varies – the juveniles have a red crown, the males a patch on the neck, while the females lack any red on the head.*

Right: *Ring-necked Parakeets are easily recognized by their bright green colouring, long tail, and also by their extremely noisy chattering calls in flight.*

WAGTAILS AND FLYCATCHERS

Both wagtails and flycatchers are largely insectivorous. Of the three species of wagtail found in the British Isles, the Yellow Wagtail is a summer visitor, as are the flycatchers.

Pied Wagtail *Motacilla alba*

Identification
A small, long-tailed, predominantly black and white bird, up to 18 cm (7 in). It walks, not hops, and constantly bobs its tail. The females and young are greyer than the males. The flight is very undulating, and they usually call in flight, a sharp disyllabic 'chis-wick'. In continental Europe, a different race occurs known as the White Wagtail, which is paler and greyer.

In the Garden
A common bird in towns and cities, often breeding on man-made structures. It roosts communally in winter, often with several hundred gathering, usually on flat-topped roofs, but also in trees. In rural areas, it is seen around farmyards, as well as rivers and streams.

Breeding
Pied Wagtails nest in holes and crevices, including drainpipes, cavities in brickwork and other similar man-made structures. They also use nest boxes. They lay 5–6

Below: *Like other wagtails, the Pied Wagtail is mainly, though not exclusively, found near water.*

Above: *Pied Wagtails are often seen in towns and cities, even in industrial sites, supermarket car parks and similar situations. They often gather in large numbers to roost on roofs or in trees.*

dark-spotted whitish eggs, which hatch after an incubation of 11–16 days, and the young fledge at about 11–16 days. When the young leave the nest, the tail is still short, but it grows rapidly once they have fledged. There are 2–3 broods a year.

Feeding
Almost entirely on small insects and other invertebrates, which they pick from the ground or in crevices. They also flycatch and hover, albeit in a rather ungainly manner.

Spotted Flycatcher *Muscicapa striata*

Identification
Up to about 14 cm (5.5 in), it is a rather nondescript bird. It is brownish with pale striations on the forehead, throat and breast, and a distinctive, relatively heavy black bill. It is most readily identified by its behaviour. It catches insects by making short sallies from a perch, such as a tree or telephone wire, and returning to the same spot.

In the Garden
A summer migrant, arriving in Britain in May and departing in late August or September. It was once a very common visitor, breeding in suburban gardens, but in the second half of the 20th century it underwent a dramatic decline, which appears to be continuing.

Breeding
Nests in cavities, including man-made structures, and readily takes to nest boxes, preferring open-fronted designs. The nest is a cup of grass, rootlets, spiders' webs and lichens lined with feathers. The Spotted Flycatcher lays 4–6 eggs, which are rather variable, but generally pale with blotches and speckling. The eggs hatch after 12–14 days, and the young fledge 12–16 days later. In fine weather there may be 2 broods.

Feeding
Almost exclusively on flying insects, but in bad weather also forages in bushes and trees.

Above: *The Spotted Flycatcher often perches on prominent branches, telegraph wires, or fences as seen here, and makes short flights to catch flying insects, returning to its perch.*

Below: *The Pied Flycatcher is mostly found in the western parts of Britain, where it occurs in mature woodland and not infrequently gardens. It often nests in boxes.*

Pied Flycatcher *Fidecula hypoleuca*

Identification
A small bird of up to 14 cm (5.5 in), the male is black above, white below with a white band on the wing. The female is pale brown instead of black. The song is variable, but generally sweet and repetitive.

In the Garden
Within its range it is often the most abundant flycatcher, and has adapted well to using nest boxes, which has undoubtedly helped increase its population. Although widespread in Europe, within the British Isles it breeds mostly in the west, and is absent from Ireland. It occurs on migration much more widely, and occasionally turns up in gardens almost anywhere.

Breeding
Nests in tree holes and hole-fronted nest boxes. Lays 4–7 pale blue eggs, which hatch after 12–13 days, and the young leave the nest 13–16 days later. There is usually only a single brood.

Feeding
It feeds almost exclusively on insects which it catches on the wing, or forages for in the canopy.

WREN AND DUNNOCK

Two small brown birds with the sexes similar in appearance, but that is about the extent of this pair's similarity. They both occur commonly in gardens. Try scattering small seeds on the ground for the Dunnock and putting out some grated cheese for the Wren.

Wren *Troglodytes troglodytes*

Identification

A small, rufous-brown bird, up to 10 cm (4 in) in length, with barring visible at close quarters. It frequently cocks its tail. It is one of the commonest birds in Britain, but its numbers drop dramatically after a hard winter. Its calls include rapid rattling notes and an abrupt, harsh 'chuck'. The song is very loud, in short high-pitched bursts lasting 4–5 seconds. During the winter months they are often the only bird singing.

In the Garden

Common and widespread, Wrens breed in many gardens, particularly if there is thick cover, such as brush piles and ivy-covered walls and hedges. They also roost in nest boxes, often communally.

Breeding

The male builds several nests in dense vegetation, such

as ivy, but also in outbuildings, and the female lays 5–8 eggs in one of the nests. The eggs are whitish and hatch 12–20 days later. The young fledge after 2–3 weeks. The other nests may be used by the young to roost in, when they have fledged and left their original nest. Wrens are polygamous.

Feeding

Wrens feed on insects and other small invertebrates, which they glean in brush piles, shrubs and tree bark.

Above: *Often looking like a brown mouse as it darts among thick vegetation, close to, the Wren's plumage can be seen to be very finely marked and barred.*

Left: *Despite its diminutive size, the Wren has a very powerful voice, and the male usually sings from a fence, shed roof top, bush or similar prominent place.*

Dunnock *Prunella modularis*

Identification
A small, insignificant bird of up to 14.5 cm (5 in), brownish above and grey below. Also known as the Hedge Sparrow, it is similar to the female House Sparrow, but with a slender bill. The song is a thin warble, quieter than either Wren or Robin.

In the Garden
Common and widespread, usually seen skulking close to the ground, or among dense vegetation.

Breeding
Nests low down in bushes and shrubs, building a cup nest of roots, twiglets and mosses, lined with hair and fine grasses. The 4–5 eggs are bright blue and hatch after 12–13 days. The young fledge after 12 days.

Feeding
The Dunnock mostly feeds on insects.

Above: *Although it is an unobtrusive bird, the Dunnock's song is remarkably attractive and powerful; it is usually delivered in short bursts, from a bush or even a telephone wire.*

Below: *The Dunnock is one of the least obtrusive birds in the garden, usually seen skulking around bushes and hiding in among the flower borders.*

THRUSHES

Thrushes are small to medium-sized birds mostly found in woodland habitats. Many species are spotted, and even those that lack spots are often spotted when in the juvenile plumage. They are generally excellent songsters, and the thrush family includes the Nightingale. Several species are long-distance migrants, and most have some seasonal movements.

Above: *The characteristic round spots of the Song Thrush can be seen clearly. Its back is also browner than the other species of thrush.*

Below: *The Redwing is a similar size to the Song Thrush but greyer on the back, with a prominent eye-stripe, and reddish under the wings.*

Song Thrush *Turdus philomelos*

Identification
Brown above, creamy below with neat brown spots, which converge into rows near the throat. It is smaller than the Blackbird, with a length of about 23 cm (9 in).

In the Garden
One of the most popular garden birds, it was once very common, but its British population underwent a dramatic decline in the second half of the 20th century. In recent years it has increased in some areas, but nowhere is it as common as it once was. It is migratory, and birds breeding in Britain move south to Spain and France, but others move in from Scandinavia and northern Europe. The song is very musical, rather fluty, with short sequences repeated two or three times.

Breeding
Song Thrushes generally have 2 or 3 broods, and build their nest in shrubs or trees. The nest is made from grasses and leaves, and lined with a smooth coating of mud. They lay 3–5 pale blue eggs, which are lightly spotted with black. They hatch in just under 2 weeks, and the young fledge 2 weeks later.

Feeding
They feed mostly on invertebrates, particularly worms and snails, smashing the latter on an 'anvil' such as a stone, drain cover or other hard object.

Redwing *Turdus iliacus*

Identification
Very similar to the Song Thrush, but slightly smaller at less than 21 cm (8.5 in), it is darker and greyer on the back, and with a prominent creamy eye-stripe. It also has a reddish patch on the flanks and underwing, which gives it its name.

In the Garden
Over most of the British Isles it is a winter visitor, but small numbers do breed. They are nocturnal migrants and their thin 'zeep' call can often be heard overhead

even in towns. They are normally present from October to March or April.

Breeding
Very rare as a breeding bird in Britain, most breed in Scandinavia and northern Russia.

Feeding
They feed mostly on berries, particularly hawthorn, but will eat rotting apples and a wide range of fruit.

Fieldfare *Turdus pilaris*

Identification
A large thrush of up to 26cm (10.5 in), heavily spotted on the underside, with a grey back to the head, brown back, grey rump and blackish tail. It is similar in size to the Mistle Thrush.

In the Garden
A winter visitor to Britain, arriving in October and staying until the following April. It is the least frequent of the thrushes in gardens – more often seen on playing fields and in parkland. But during hard weather, particularly when there is snow cover, it can be a visitor.

Breeding
Small numbers have bred in Britain since the 1960s, but it is still very rare and unlikely to be encountered.

Feeding
On open fields the Fieldfare feeds on earthworms and other invertebrates, but also visits hedgerows to feed on berries, and will readily take rotting apples and other fruit in gardens.

Mistle Thrush *Turdus viscivorus*

Identification
This large bird is up to 27 cm (11 in) in length, with a boldly spotted underside. It is often seen singing from the tops of very tall trees, often in inclement weather.

In the Garden
Widespread, it often occurs in town centres where there are parks and squares with large trees. In winter, numbers are augmented by migrants from Scandinavia.

Breeding
Nests in early March to July, building a cup-shaped nest

Above: *The Fieldfare is a large thrush which, although small numbers now stay to breed in Britain, is a winter visitor, often occurring in large flocks.*

from grasses and other vegetation. Lays 3–5 eggs which are blue-green, speckled with brown. The eggs hatch after an incubation of 12–15 days, and the young fledge 12–16 days later. It usually has 2 broods.

Feeding
The Mistle Thrush will feed mostly on the ground, taking insects, grubs, earthworms and other invertebrates. In winter they will feed on rotting fruit.

Below: *The Mistle Thrush is a similar size to the Fieldfare but more uniformly coloured. Like other thrushes, in winter it is often attracted to feed on rotting apples.*

Above: *Blackbirds are perhaps one of the most common and widespread of garden birds, but the male which is almost entirely black, with a yellow bill, is a striking and beautiful bird.*

Blackbird *Turdus merula*

Identification
Up to 25 cm (10 in) in length, the Blackbird shows strong sexual dimorphism – the males are jet-black and the females are dark brown. The juveniles are like the females but more spotted. It has a musical song.

In the Garden
Widespread over much of Europe, and one of the most familiar of all garden birds, occurring in almost every garden in Britain, and breeding throughout suburban and urban areas.

Breeding
Blackbirds build their nest in a tree or bush, and if suitable sites are not available, they have been known to build on a variety of man-made structures. They can have up to 5 broods in a year. The nest is made from grasses and other vegetation, and will also include paper in urban areas. It lays 3–5 pale blue, heavily freckled eggs. They hatch about 2 weeks later, and the young fledge after another 2 weeks.

Feeding
They feed mostly on earthworms and other invertebrates, but will also feed on household scraps, such as bread and fruit.

Robin *Erithacus rubecula*

Identification
A small thrush of up to 14 cm (5.5 in), it is usually claimed as Britain's national bird, and is found over most of Europe. The adults are easily identified by the bright orange-red breast. The juveniles are quite different, and are more like a miniature juvenile Blackbird – they are dull spotted brown. The Robin's song is thin and fluty, and their call is a metallic 'tic- tic-tic'.

In the Garden
Common in most gardens, Robins also often become very tame, following a gardener around to snatch earthworms and grubs. With patience they can be tamed fairly readily to take food from the hand. Although resident, numbers are also augmented by migrants during the winter.

Breeding
They nest in cavities, but not holes, also inside sheds and outbuildings, and open-fronted nest boxes are preferred. The female lays 3–5 pale greenish, spotted with brownish red, eggs. They hatch after 12–15 days and the young fledge 12–15 days later. There are up to 5 broods.

Feeding
Primarily insectivorous, feeding on insects, grubs and other invertebrates. Robins will feed at bird tables, particularly if live food is available. They also take tadpoles and fish fry occasionally.

Below: *The Robin, Britain's national bird, is extremely intolerant and aggressive, driving away others of the same sex and species. However, it can also become very tame and confiding.*

Above: *The Black Redstart is a common garden bird in many parts of continental Europe, but in Britain it is mostly found in industrial sites, such as power stations and factory yards.*

Black Redstart *Phoenicurus ochrurus*

Identification
A Robin-sized bird, 14 cm (5.5 in) in length, which is mostly dark grey, with a rufous tail. It has a powerful song often heard above the din of industrial sites.

In the Garden
In Britain, Black Redstarts are very unusual in gardens, but small numbers do breed in urban locations. After World War II many bombed sites were colonized and they subsequently bred in industrial sites, such as power stations and warehouses. In continental Europe, they are often common in gardens, particularly in alpine areas. They are partial migrants. Their song can often be heard above the noise of industrial sites, high on rooftops, with distinctive metallic sounds.

Breeding
They nest in cavities, often in masonry. They lay 4–6 eggs, which hatch after 12–17 days and the young fledge 16–18 days later.

Feeding
They are almost exclusively insectivorous.

Redstart *Phoenicurus phoenicurus*

Identification
Up to 14 cm (5.5 in) in length, the male is spectacular, rich orange-brown on the underside, with a jet-black throat and nape, and pure white crown. The start of the tail is reddish. The female is much duller, but has a reddish tail. It has a ticking alarm call. The song, which often starts before dawn, is rather Chaffinch-like, delivered from a treetop.

In the Garden
Now a rare visitor to gardens, but in some areas it does occur and will readily breed in suitable nest boxes. It is usually associated with mature woodland, open parkland or wooded heaths. It is a summer visitor.

Breeding
Redstarts nest in cavities and when they use nest boxes, often choose open fronted boxes as well as boxes with holes. They lay 6–7 eggs, which are pale blue. The eggs hatch after 11–14 days and the young fledge 14–20 days later.

Feeding
They are almost exclusively insectivorous and not common visitors to feeders.

Below: *The male Redstart in breeding plumage is one of the most beautiful birds in Europe. The species has declined dramatically and is now rare.*

WARBLERS

Warblers are mostly summer visitors, although two species (Blackcap and Chiffchaff) winter in small numbers. Warblers are all primarily insectivorous, but in autumn several species feed extensively on soft fruits such as blackberries. Their name derives from the fact that many of them have attractive songs, although some, such as the Grasshopper Warbler, have very monotonous songs. Several of the warblers are LBJs (Little Brown Jobs) par excellence, and among the most difficult of birds to identify, particularly in autumn, when juveniles and migrants occur.

Willow Warbler *Phylloscopus trochilus*

Identification
A small, 11.5 cm (4.5 in), greenish warbler, it is pale yellowish white on the underside with a yellowish eye-stripe, and pinkish legs. Its song is a fluty descending, accelerating scale. The song might be confused with that of the Chaffinch, which is more rattling.

In the Garden
A common summer visitor, arriving in late April and leaving in August/September. It is common in larger gardens in suburban and rural areas, often, as its name suggests, associated with willows.

Breeding
Nests close to the ground, in thick vegetation, laying 4–8 eggs, which are whitish, with fine speckling. The eggs hatch after 12–14 days and the young fledge after 11–15 days. Occasionally there is a second brood in the south of their range. In recent years, numbers have declined, but this may be due to problems in the wintering habitat in Africa.

Feeding
They are exclusively insectivorous, picking small insects and grubs from vegetation, and sometimes flycatching.

Chiffchaff *Phylloscopus collybita*

Identification
Superficially very similar to the Willow Warbler, the famous parson-naturalist Gilbert White was one of the first to distinguish this species in the field. It is 11 cm (4–4.5 in) long, slightly greyer than the Willow Warbler, and usually has grey legs. It is easily identified by its song, which is a loud and oft-repeated 'chiff-chaff', often heard high in the canopy of the trees where it feeds.

In the Garden
The Chiffchaff is not uncommon in suburban and rural gardens, notably during spring and autumn migration. In southern England many winter in gardens. Most, however, are summer visitors, arriving in March or April and leaving by September.

Breeding
The nest is well-hidden and built close to the ground, often at the base of a tree or shrub, in thick

Left: *The Willow Warbler nests close to the ground in dense vegetation, and the male has a distinctive melodious, descending song.*

Left: *The Chiffchaff has an onomatopoeic song, heard very early in spring. A few individuals remain in Britain all the year, but most are migratory.*

Below: *In winter, the unmistakable Goldcrest with its brilliant golden crown, frequently feeds in ivy, which attracts insects to its flowers. When feeding this tiny bird often hovers like a hummingbird.*

vegetation. They lay 4–7 whitish eggs that have a few dark spots. The eggs hatch after 13–15 days, and the young leave the nest 12–15 days later. Chiffchaffs often have 2 broods.

Feeding
They feed mostly on small insects, but also take blackberries and other fruit in autumn. At feeders they will take crushed peanuts and other seeds.

winter they often move into suburban areas, mixed with Long-tailed and other tits.

Breeding
They build a nest from mosses, lichens and other vegetation held together with spiders' webs, and usually in a fork at the end of a branch. They usually have 2 broods and lay 7–12 very tiny eggs, which are whitish with fine spotting. They hatch after about 16 days and the young leave the nest about 19 days later.

Feeding
They feed on tiny insects and spiders, picked off leaves and branches.

Goldcrest *Regulus regulus*

Identification
Very closely related to the Willow Warblers, it is 9 cm (3.5 in), greenish olive above and whitish below, and instantly recognizable by the brilliant crown stripe. It is golden yellow, bordered on both sides with black. The Goldcrest is only likely to be confused with the Firecrest, which is far less common, and has a pale eye-stripe.

In the Garden
Not uncommon in gardens, particularly in winter, when it often mixes with tits, Treecreepers and warblers. It has an extremely high-pitched call, 'zee-zee-zee'. In flight, Goldcrests often hover, like hummingbirds. They often forage high up in trees, and also in dense cover, such as Leyland Cypress. In

Blackcap *Sylvia atricapilla*

Identification

A relatively large warbler of up to 13 cm (5 in), with mainly grey plumage. The male has a black cap, the females and young have a chestnut-brown cap. The underparts are slightly paler than the back. The song of the male is a very melodious warble, very similar indeed to the Garden Warbler, but generally in shorter phrases, and with a wider range of pitch. They usually sing well hidden in the middle of a bush or tree.

In the Garden

A common summer visitor, with small numbers wintering in the British Isles, particularly in southern England. It is found in larger gardens especially in rural areas, and near parkland.

Breeding

They nest in dense shrubs, building a cup-shaped nest, and laying 4–6 eggs, pale buff with fine spotting. The eggs hatch after about 10–12 days, and the young fledge 10–13 days later. They may have 2 broods.

Feeding

They are mostly insectivorous, but in autumn they feed extensively on fruit, particularly blackberries, and will visit feeders.

Garden Warbler
Sylvia borin

Identification

One of the most nondescript small birds, with almost no obvious distinguishing features, the Garden Warbler is relatively large for a warbler at 14 cm (5.5 in). It is brownish above, paler

Below: A male Blackcap – distinguished from his mate by the cap, which is rufous-brown in the female. An increasing number of these summer migrants now winter in southern England.

Above: A female Blackcap which, like the juveniles, has a brown cap. Similar to most small birds, the Blackcap is attracted to water in a garden.

below, and the sexes are very similar. Its song is very attractive and melodious, but difficult to distinguish from that of the Blackcap.

In the Garden
A summer visitor, arriving in May, and departing in August, it prefers dense shrubby vegetation and woodland. It is not usually found in urban gardens but is not uncommon in larger rural gardens. Like many other migrants numbers are also controlled by weather conditions in Africa.

Breeding
Builds a cup-shaped nest in a fork in shrubs or low bushes, from dry grasses, moss and fine twigs and lined with rootlets and hair. Lays 4–5 eggs which are whitish, variable with blotching and speckling. They hatch after 11–12 days, and the young leave the nest 9–10 days later. Sometimes there are 2 broods.

Feeding
Mostly insectivorous, Garden Warblers eat fruit and berries in autumn.

Above: *The Garden Warbler is best identified by its lack of any distinguishing features. However, the male does have a very attractive warbling song, very similar to that of the Blackcap.*

Below: *The male Whitethroat has a characteristic white bib, and often sings from the top of bushes, fences or telephone wires, usually making a short flight while in song.*

Whitethroat *Sylvia communis*

Identification
A large warbler at 14 cm (5.5 in), brown on the back, paler below, with a white chin, and, in the male, a grey head. The female is duller. Both sexes have white outer tail feathers, which are often visible in flight. Their song is very distinctive and usually delivered from a prominent perch, or in flight, and is a brief, rather scratchy warble.

In the Garden
Summer migrants, Whitethroats typically occur in woodland edge and hedgerow habitats, but are also found in garden hedges in more rural areas, and occur in suburban gardens on migration. Their numbers underwent a catastrophic decline in the last half of the 20th century owing to adverse conditions in their wintering grounds in Africa, but numbers have slowly recovered.

Breeding
They nest in hedges and bushes, and lay 4–5

dark-spotted, pale eggs, which hatch after 11–14 days incubation, and the young fledge 10–12 days later; they often rear 2 broods.

Feeding
They are insectivorous, but in autumn feed extensively on blackberries and other fruit.

TITS

Small, largely insectivorous birds, often very brightly coloured. Originally known as tit-mice or tomtits, 'tit' being a diminutive prefix, it also applied to other birds such as titlark. Most species are hole nesters and have readily adapted to the man-made environment, and they are all popular at bird feeders.

Above: *A Blue Tit, easily identified by its small size, and bright cerulean blue colouring. The newly fledged young are much more yellow than the adults.*

Left: *Blue Tits are among the commonest and most abundant visitors to bird feeders, and are attracted by peanuts, suet and a wide variety of other foods.*

Blue Tit *Parus caeruleus*

Identification
An unmistakable, small, agile bird up to 11.5 cm (4.5 in). The head, wings and tail are a bright cerulean blue, and the back greenish blue, the face white and the underparts yellow. There is a blue stripe running through the eye, and an indistinct blue stripe in the centre of the belly. The adults have white cheeks, but the newly fledged young are yellowish. It has a wide range of chattering calls and its song is described as 'tsee-tsee-tsee-chu-chu-chu'. They also have a churring alarm call, and many other trills and churring sounds.

In the Garden
Very widespread and one of the commonest birds in most suburban gardens. It readily breeds in nest boxes and during the winter months travels from feeder to feeder in small flocks, often mixed with other species. Observations of ringed birds have shown that what appears to be a dozen or so individuals in a garden may in fact be up to 100 visitors.

Breeding
Blue Tits nest in tree holes, crevices in brickwork and also nest boxes – in fact the latter provide the majority of nest sites in many suburban areas. The nest is made from mosses and grass, and lined with feathers. They lay up to 16 eggs, which hatch after 13–16 days, and the young fledge 16–22 days later.

Feeding
They feed mostly on caterpillars, grubs and other small invertebrates when they are available. In winter, Blue Tits search for insects in bark and other crevices, but also feed extensively at feeders. They particularly like peanuts, suet, coconut and other foods with a very high fat content.

Great Tit *Parus major*

Identification
Up to 14.5 cm (5 in) in length, it is larger than the Blue Tit. The Great Tit is black on the head, contrasting with white cheeks and has a black stripe running down the centre of the yellow underparts. The stripe of the male is much wider than that of the female. The young birds have creamy yellow cheeks. Great Tits have an amazingly wide range of calls, but the most familiar is a repeated call of 'teacher-teacher'.

In the Garden
Very widespread and nearly as abundant as the Blue Tit, occurring in most gardens. After a series of mild winters numbers tend to be high, but like those of many other small birds, populations crash whenever there is a long freeze.

Breeding
Nests in cavities, including nest boxes, making its nest from grasses, mosses and leaves lined with feathers. It lays up to 11 eggs, which hatch after 11–15 days of incubation. The young fledge about 3 weeks later. Sometimes there is a second brood.

Feeding
Like other tits, Great Tits feed mostly on insect larvae and other small invertebrates, but they have also adapted to visiting bird feeders and are particularly fond of peanuts and sunflower seeds.

Above: A male Great Tit, distinguished from the female by having a much broader black stripe down the centre of the belly.

Below: The Crested Tit is easily distinguished from all other tit species by its crest. In Britain it is confined to the coniferous forests of Scotland.

Breeding
Similar to other tits, Crested Tits nest in tree holes and will also use nest boxes. They lay 5–8 white, slightly speckled eggs, which hatch after 13–18 days and fledge 17–21 days later.

Feeding
They feed mostly on insects and spiders gleaned from conifers. They also come to feeders in winter.

Crested Tit *Parus cristatus*

Identification
A small tit, 12 cm (5 in) in length, with a very obvious crest. Its colouring is otherwise rather dingey. It spends much of the day feeding in the canopy and can best be detected by its high-pitched trilling calls.

In the Garden
Widespread, particularly in mountainous areas of Europe, but in Britain, confined to a relatively small area of Scotland. They are closely associated with coniferous forests, but like other tits, within their range are often frequent visitors to gardens.

Above: *The Marsh Tit is a less frequent visitor to gardens than the Great, Blue or Coal Tit. It is rather dull in colouring and may be confused with the male Blackcap.*

Marsh Tit *Parus palustris*

Identification
At 11.5 cm (4.5 in), the Marsh Tit is midway in body size between the Blue and Great Tits. It is greyish overall with a black cap. The sides of the head are whitish, and the underside pinkish-grey, and upperparts grey. It is very similar to the less widespread Willow Tit, and most easily distinguished by its call. The Marsh Tit's call is a whistling 'pitch-oo', or 'chew-chew-chew', and the Willow's is a more nasal 'chay-chay-chay'. They can also be confused with the male Blackcap, which is larger and more slender, with a longer bill.

In the Garden
Marsh Tits are not uncommon visitors to bird feeders, but never as common as Great and Blue Tits. They are more common in gardens near to woodlands and forests.

Breeding
The Marsh Tit nests in holes building a cup of mosses and lined with hair and feathers. It lays 6–9 white eggs speckled with red-brown, which are incubated for 13–17 days and the young fledge after 16–21 days in the nest. Usually a single brood, sometimes 2 in the south of their range.

Feeding
Like other tits it is primarily insectivorous, feeding on grubs of insects and other invertebrates, but it is also a regular visitor to feeders, particularly to suet.

Coal Tit *Parus ater*

Identification
A small tit of up to 11.5 cm (4.5 in) long, it is similar in size to the Blue Tit, pinkish grey below, grey on the back, with a black cap and black chin. It has a characteristic white patch on the back of the head. The calls are high-pitched, most likely to be confused with a Goldcrest.

In the Garden
Widespread and locally a common bird in gardens, particularly near to conifer plantations, or even in gardens with conifers. Like other tits, it often occurs in mixed flocks in winter.

Breeding
Coal Tits nest in holes, often close to the ground, but will occupy hole-fronted nest boxes. They lay 7-9 eggs, which are whitish, with some light speckling, and which hatch after 13-18 days. The young fledge 16-22 days later.

Feeding
Mostly insectivorous, feeding on insects and spiders gleaned from conifers in summer, they readily take to bird feeders, feeding on suet and peanuts.

Below: *The Coal Tit is similar to the Marsh Tit, but has a white 'window' on the back of the head.*

Long-tailed Tit
Aegithalos longicaudatus

Identification
The smallest of the tits, but has a very long tail, giving it a total length of up to 14 cm (5.5 in). Its black, white and pink colouring is distinctive. It is almost invariably seen in flocks outside the breeding season, sometimes mixed with tits, crests and other species. It is very noisy, making a wide range of contact calls, including a very high-pitched 'tsee-tsee-tsee'. This sound can be imitated by whistling through the teeth, and the birds will often crowd around for a few minutes. They can also be attracted by jangling keys, shaking coins together and 'pishing'.

In the Garden
A familiar visitor to many gardens, particularly in winter, when flocks move into suburbs from more rural areas. The families stay together during the winter, and sometimes two or more join up to form larger flocks. They are rather restless, forever on the move, and although they are regular visitors to feeders they often move on after a short while.

Above: *The diminutive Long-tailed Tit is one of the most popular of all birds visiting bird feeders, and in winter usually occurs in flocks of half a dozen or more.*

Below: *The Long-tailed Tit forms flocks in winter, but in summer the pair will build a domed nest in large shrubs or bushes. They use spider's webs to hold the nest together.*

Breeding
Unlike other tits, the Long-tailed Tit does not nest in holes, but builds a domed nest, made of mosses, lichens and other vegetation, bound together with spiders' webs, and lined with feathers. It is usually built in dense shrubbery. They lay up to 12 tiny, finely spotted, white eggs, which hatch after 13–17 days' incubation, and the young fledge after 15–17 days.

Feeding
It feeds almost exclusively on small insects, grubs and spiders, and also comes to feeders where it is fond of suet, but will also feed on peanuts.

NUTHATCH AND TREECREEPER

These birds are not closely related and look very different from each other, but they both feed on tree-trunks and branches. The Treecreeper, with its long, thin, probing bill, is largely insectivorous. The Nuthatch has a strong bill capable of cracking nuts. The Nuthatch is more likely to visit feeding stations.

Treecreeper *Certhia familiaris*

Identification
A small, brown bird, 12.5 cm (5 in) long, with mottled brown plumage above, whitish below, and with a long slender, downward curving bill. It runs up tree-trunks, but always flies down to start again, and is rather mouse-like in its movements. Its call is high-pitched, and its song is rather wren-like, but not as strident.

In the Garden
Although widespread, it is most likely to be seen in larger gardens, or gardens close to woodlands or parks. In winter it is sometimes seen in mixed flocks of tits and crests. They are unobstrusive birds, easily overlooked.

Breeding
They build their nests in clefts and crevices in tree bark, and will adapt to specially designed nest boxes. The nest is built from mosses, lined with hair and feathers, and they lay 5–6 eggs which are white with fine brown spotting. The eggs hatch after 13–15 days and the young fledge 14–16 days later.

Feeding
Treecreepers feed on small invertebrates, which they pick from crevices in bark. They are rare on bird feeders, but do sometimes visit, particularly after prolonged frosts.

Left: *The Treecreeper is a bird that is easily overlooked. It runs up trees like a mouse, but is well camouflaged. It prefers larger gardens with mature trees.*

Below: *The Treecreeper probes bark crevices with its bill for insects and spiders. Its long, stiff tail helps the bird balance in an upright position against the bark.*

Nuthatch *Sitta europaea*

Identification

An unmistakable, small bird, measuring about 14 cm (5.5 in) in length, it is blue-grey above and pinkish buff below, with a dagger-like bill and a black eye-stripe. The Nuthatch is disimilar to woodpeckers and the Treecreeper, in the fact that it climbs tree-trunks both up and down. Its calls are very variable and include a loud piping 'whit-whit'.

In the Garden

The Nuthatch is widespread and is often a regular visitor to gardens, particularly gardens that are in the neighbourhood of woodlands and parklands.

Breeding

Nuthatches nest in old woodpecker holes and occasionally nest boxes. They plaster the entrance with mud to reduce the size of the opening and therefore exclude larger birds such as Starlings. They lay 6–9 eggs, sometimes as many as 13, which are white with some reddish speckling. They hatch after 14–18 days and the young fledge at 23–25 days. They produce one brood.

Feeding

They feed on insects and grubs, which they hunt in crevices, and also extensively on berries and nuts. They wedge nuts in crevices and hammer them open. They are regular visitors to feeders and are fond of peanuts and other nuts. They also hoard food in anticipation of winter weather.

Below: *Being nut feeders, Nuthatches are relatively easy to attract to bird feeders with peanuts. Unlike woodpeckers, Nuthatches can climb up and down trees.*

Above: *The Nuthatch, despite its small size, uses its powerful beak to smash open nuts. It wedges larger ones such as hazels in cracks in tree bark.*

STARLING AND CROWS

Crows are a family of relatively large birds, generally considered to be more intelligent than most other birds. Although many crow species are uniformly black, some of them are among the more colourfully plumaged birds. In the past all species of crow in the British Isles were persecuted by gamekeepers, and the Raven and Chough are still rare. The Raven was once widespread in and around London and the home counties – with lots of evidence for its distribution in place names that include 'raven'. But now it is confined to remote areas. It is an ideal candidate for reintroduction to its former habitats. With the reduction in persecution, other crows have all increased. However, they are all extensively trapped and shot, and in some parts of the country, such as East Anglia, it is still possible to see corpses dangling from sticks as a 'deterrent' to others.

Starling *Sturnus vulgaris*

Identification
Smaller than a Blackbird of up to 21 cm (8.5 in), from a distance it appears dark. However, at close quarters, it is a spectacularly plumaged bird. In summer its head and underside are blue-black with sheens of purple and green, contrasting with a pointed yellow bill, and in winter it develops extensive pale spotting. The juvenile is a dull brown. Starlings have a rather upright stance and walk; they do not hop. They mimic a wide range of sounds – telephones ringing being frequent – and it is

Below: The Starling is one of the most common birds in towns and villages, and a regular visitor to gardens. In winter plumage, it has characteristic pale spotting.

not uncommon for Starlings to imitate Curlews, having learned the call while wintering in marshlands. In addition they have a wide range of wheezing, whistling and chattering calls.

In the Garden
A common and widespread species, with numbers augmented in winter with migrants from Scandinavia and Russia. In winter Starlings form large flocks – sometimes gathering in numbers of 250,000 or more to roost. They roost in towns on window ledges and trees, and also in reed beds.

Breeding
They are hole nesters, using old woodpecker holes, natural cavities, and also nesting under eaves and in larger nest boxes. They lay 1 or 2 clutches of 4–7 pale

Above: *A male Starling in song. Close to, the beautiful iridescent plumage can be seen, and the male's song is full of mimicry – even mobile phones are now common.*

Above: *Magpies are attractive and intelligent birds, but most people do not like them because they predate on small birds, and their eggs and nestlings.*

blue, unmarked eggs, which hatch after 12–15 days, and the young fledge 20–22 days later.

and the young fledge 22–28 days later.

Feeding
They feed mostly on the ground, but will also use feeders and bird tables. They eat largely invertebrates, particularly grubs, but also a very wide range of other foods.

Feeding
They are omnivores, feeding on insects, household scraps, as well as carrion from road kills. During the spring and summer months they also feed extensively on the eggs and young of small birds.

Magpie *Pica pica*

Identification
An unmistakable, black and white bird with a long tail, up to 48 cm (19 in) long. In fact the black colouring is iridescent, with green, blue and purple sheens. The sexes are similar. The call is a harsh chattering rattle, and Magpies often give the alarm to other birds at the approach of human or feline and other intruders.

In the Garden
Very common and widespread in Europe, and also occurs in North America. In Britain, by the end of the 19th century, it had been reduced to very low numbers and was generally exceedingly shy. This was because it was extensively persecuted by gamekeepers. In the last quarter of the 20th century it is estimated that its numbers trebled in the British Isles. Outside the breeding season, it is often seen in parties of up to 15–20.

Breeding
It builds a stick nest, sometimes in a thorn bush or other dense cover, or in an obvious position near a treetop. They lay a single clutch of 5–8 blue-green eggs which are blotched with brown. The eggs hatch after 18 days,

Below: *Magpies are generally seen in ones and twos, but occasionally in small flocks, usually the adults with their young.*

123

Jay *Garrulus glandarius*

Identification

A very noisy bird, with a harsh, grating call, it is often heard before it is seen. It is fairly large at about 34 cm (14 in) and brightly coloured. Most of the body is pinkish buff, with black and white wings and tail, a black patch either side of the bill and bright blue 'wrist'. The feathers are bright sky-blue with fine black barring. In flight, the wings are very rounded and a white rump is conspicuous.

Above: *The brightly coloured Jay is very shy, but often found in larger gardens and parks. In autumn Jays move around, sometimes in small flocks, in search of acorns.*

Below: *At rest the blue and black feathers on the Jay's wing are partly concealed.*

In the Garden

Common in most gardens, at least as an occasional visitor. Usually nesting in larger gardens, parkland and woods. During the breeding season it is very shy and easily overlooked, but in autumn, it is often conspicuous and seen flying between feeding areas.

Breeding

It builds a stick nest, usually in a hawthorn or other dense tree or bush, laying 5–8 eggs, which are pale with dark freckling. The eggs hatch after 16–17 days and the young fledge 19–23 days later.

Feeding

Omnivorous, eating insects, grubs, as well as fruits and berries. In autumn, Jays feed extensively on acorns, which they also bury. In spring and summer, they take the eggs and young of small birds.

Carrion Crow *Corvus corone*

Identification

A large, 47 cm (18.5 in), glossy black bird, with a black bill; the closely related Rook has a thinner bill and whitish-grey face and is generally confined to more rural areas. The Hooded Crow was until recently regarded as a subspecies of the Carrion Crow. Although they are now regarded as two separate species and are very different in appearance, in other respects they are rather similar.

In the Garden

Once very rare and shy, owing to persecution by gamekeepers, the Carrion Crow is now widespread and often common. It nests in parks and larger gardens and is a frequent visitor to all gardens. However, because of its depredations on the nests of smaller birds, it is generally not welcomed. It is still considered a serious pest by gamekeepers and may be legally shot and trapped.

Breeding

Carrion Crows build a bulky nest of twigs, with scant lining. They lay a single clutch of 4-6 eggs, which are pale blue-green with dark blotches.

Above: *Despite persecution by gamekeepers, Carrion Crows are now widespread, even in towns and cities.*

Above: *The noisy and sociable Carrion Crow is all black with a powerful black bill.*

The eggs hatch after 17–21 days and the young fledge at 4–5 weeks.

Feeding
Truly omnivorous and a scavenger, as its name suggests. Feeds extensively on roadkills and visits garbage dumps.

Jackdaw *Corvus monedula*

Identification
A small, 33 cm (13 in) crow, predominantly grey with a black cap and a bright blue-grey eye. Like most other crows, the sexes are similar. The call is a nasal 'jack'.

In the Garden
Once widespread even in towns and cities, it is still fairly common in rural and suburban areas, although much more rarely found in urban areas. Jackdaws have benefited from the trend to keep pigs in extensive conditions and as a result, they are able to raid the pigs' food supplies. Jackdaws are famed for collecting brightly coloured objects, such as keys and rings, which they take to their nests.

Breeding
Colonial hole nesters, Jackdaws were often associated with church towers, as well as ruined castles and other man-made structures. However, many churches and cathedrals have now made the towers inaccessible to nesting birds. They nest in tree hollows and will adapt to nest boxes. They lay 4–6 pale blue, heavily freckled eggs, which hatch after 17–18 days and the young fledge about 28–32 days later.

Feeding
Omnivores, feeding on a wide range of small animals, including grubs and other invertebrates, but also carrion and they will raid birds' nests for eggs and young.

Below: *The Jackdaw is a hole-nesting species. Although once common in most towns and cities, it has declined because old trees have been felled and church belfries blocked with netting.*

125

SPARROWS, FINCHES AND BUNTINGS

Small, often seed-eating birds, they show a remarkable range of plumages, and occupy a very wide range of habitats. Many are occasional visitors to gardens, and in the past often occurred in very large flocks. In winter mixed flocks of finches used to gather on stubbles and other fields to feed on weed seeds, but the intensification of agriculture has largely banished such sights, and many species may be dependent on bird feeding in suburban areas for their future survival.

House Sparrow *Passer domesticus*

Identification
A familiar small brown bird, up to 15 cm (6 in). The male has a grey crown, chestnut nape and a black bib and white cheeks. The females and young are much duller. The song is a repeated chirping.

In the Garden
One of the most familiar birds, widespread and often abundant. It is a true commensal, rarely found away from human habitations. However, from being a major pest at the beginning of the 20th century, at the beginning of the 21st century, it had disappeared from many areas, and continues to decline. The reasons are not understood, but the lack of insects during the breeding season is thought to be a factor. The Tree Sparrow has also undergone a similar decline, and is even rarer.

Breeding
Normally nests in cavities, under eaves, under loose tiles and in similar places. Nest boxes designed for sparrows are now available. House Sparrows occasionally nest in hedges, and build an untidy nest that betrays their relationship with weaverbirds. They lay 3–6 eggs, which are buff, with fine speckling, and hatch after about 11–14 days. The young fledge 14–19 days later. They can raise 3 or 4 broods a year.

Feeding
In summer they feed mostly on small insects, and at other times of the year on seeds, including grain. They are regular visitors to feeders, particularly for peanuts and seeds.

Above: *The female House Sparrow is much duller than her mate. Sparrows have a hopping gait, and a cheerful chirruping call. There have been dramatic declines in most urban populations, which are unexplained.*

Left: *The male House Sparrow is easily recognized by his black bib. The Tree Sparrow has a black spot on the cheeks.*

Chaffinch *Fringilla coelebs*

Identification
The Chiffchaff is a similar size to the House Sparrow – 15 cm (6 in) – but it has a lighter build and a thinner bill. The male has a pink underside contrasting with a greyish blue top to the head and nape. The female is much duller, but both sexes have prominent white patches on the wings, which are particularly obvious in flight. The call is a metallic 'pink pink', and the male's song a trilling descending scale ending in a flourish.

In the Garden
One of the most widespread birds in Europe and common in gardens throughout. Chaffinches are typical birds of woodland and woodland-edge habitats, and flourish in hedges and suburban gardens.

Breeding
The males establish territories and start singing in the canopy in February or March. The nest is a shallow cup made from small twigs, mosses and other vegetation, lined with hair and feathers. They lay 3–5 eggs, pale blue with a few dark spots, which hatch after 11–13 days, and the young fledge 12–15 days later. They normally have a single brood, occasionally a second.

Feeding
They feed on insects and grubs during the breeding season, but the rest of the year on seeds and berries. They frequently feed on the ground, but also visit bird tables, and also feeders.

Above: *Close up, the amazing range of colours in the plumage of the male Chaffinch can be seen. In winter Chaffinches usually gather in flocks, and prefer to feed on the ground.*

Breeding
They nest in Scandinavia.

Feeding
They feed mostly on seeds, grain and, in particular, beech mast.

Below: *Similar in size and behaviour to the Chaffinch, the Brambling is a winter visitor to the British Isles and usually seen in flocks.*

Brambling *Fringilla montifringilla*

Identification
Similar in size to the Chaffinch, the Brambling is 15 cm (6 in), with orange and black plumage, and a characteristic black-tipped, yellowish bill. When it flies away, the pure white rump is exposed.

In the Garden
A winter migrant, breeding in Scandinavia, although it has bred sporadically in Britain. Once not uncommon in suburban and rural gardens but, like many birds that feed on farmlands on grain and weed seeds, Bramblings have decreased significantly. In some years they are abundant, usually found close to beech woods. They are often seen in mixed flocks with Chaffinches and other finches.

Above: *With rather a fine bill for a finch, the Siskin has attractive, yellowish-green plumage. They are readily attracted to feeding on peanuts, particularly those in red plastic nets.*

Below: *Greenfinches are common at bird feeders, but can be very aggressive, driving away other birds, such as the Great Tit seen here.*

Siskin *Carduelis spinus*

Identification
A small, slender finch, up to 12 cm (5 in), with a small pointed bill, and a forked tail. The male is more brightly coloured than the female and has yellowish-green, streaked plumage, with a prominent yellow patch on blackish wings and a black forehead. The females are generally duller and browner. They have a range of twittering calls.

In the Garden
Siskins generally occur in small flocks in winter, particularly in late winter, when natural food supplies have been exhausted.

Breeding
They nest in coniferous forests.

Feeding
In gardens they are famous for having a preference for feeding on peanuts in red plastic nets. However, they also take a range of other foods. They generally move in small flocks settling for a few minutes then moving on.

Greenfinch *Carduelis chloris*

Identification
A relatively large, robust finch, up to 15 cm (6 in), with a powerful pale-coloured bill. The overall colouring is greyish green and olive-green, with yellow patches on the wing. They vary considerably, the adult males being brightest, and the young females dullest. They have a characteristic wheezing call.

In the Garden
Greenfinches are common and widespread in gardens, both as breeding birds, and also in winter. They are particularly aggressive, often driving away other birds while they are on feeders. They also form mixed flocks with other finches and sparrows, which in the past could often number several hundred, though such flocks are now rare.

Breeding

They nest in shrubs, bushes and trees, sometimes in small, loose colonies. The nest is a shallow cup of twigs, roots and mosses lined with hair and feathers. They lay 3–6 pale, dark-spotted eggs, which hatch after 12–14 days. The young fledge 13–17 days later.

Feeding

Greenfinches feed largely on seeds, but feed the young on insects, and in winter eat nuts and seeds at feeders.

Goldfinch
Carduelis carduelis

Identification

A lightly built 14 cm (5.5 in) finch, with spectacular colouring. The sexes are similar, with a bright red face surrounded with a white band, and black back to the head. The wings are black and golden yellow. The body colour is a pale buff. The juveniles lack the red face. In flight they have a twittering call, and they are generally seen perched on the tops of bushes, thistles and other tall plants.

In the Garden

Common and widespread, nesting in hedges and in other open habitats. The Goldfinch visits suburban gardens in winter, usually in a small flock, and it sometimes mixes with other finches. Like many other finches, it was once trapped in large numbers to be kept as a caged bird.

Breeding

They build a cup-shaped nest, often at the end of a branch, made from mosses and lichens, and grasses. They lay 4-6 pale bluish eggs, finely spotted and streaked with purplish black, which hatch after 12–14 days, and the young fledge 12–15 days later. They usually lay 2 clutches, occasionally 3.

Feeding

Goldfinches feed mostly on seeds and are particularly fond of thistle seeds. They can also be attracted by planting teasel.

Above: *Goldfinches are among the most colourful of European birds, and were once captured in their thousands as cage birds. One of their favourite foods is the seed of teasels.*

Below: *Goldfinches are regular visitors to bird tables, often in small flocks – appropriately known as a 'charm'. They feed on thistle, niger and other small seeds.*

Left: *Redpolls are not common in gardens, but do occasionally visit, particularly during cold weather. They are often found close to water, and like willows and alders.*

only found in gardens during the winter months, when they are usually in small flocks, sometimes mixed with Siskins. They often feed on birch and alder.

Breeding
Redpolls have a northerly breeding range, nesting in loose colonies.

Feeding
In the breeding season they are largely insectivorous and in winter feed on seeds. They feed on the ground, as well as in trees, and also regularly visit feeders. They are often attracted to water.

Redpoll *Carduelis flammea*

Identification
A small, fork-tailed finch, up to 13 cm (5 in), it is very similar to the Linnet, but darker with a more heavily streaked plumage. The male has a bright pink patch on the forehead, from which it takes its name, but the female is much duller. Both sexes have a small black bib, and two pale wing bars, and a pale rump visible in flight.

In the Garden
Widespread in Britain and northern Europe. Generally

Linnet *Carduelis cannabina*

Identification
A small, prettily coloured finch, up to14 cm (5.5 in). The male is greyish with brown wings, a pink breast and pink patch on the forehead. The female is much duller, and both sexes have a characteristic forked tail and white outer tail feathers, and white on the wings. It has a twittering flight call.

In the Garden
Once a very common and widespread bird particularly in farmland, its numbers have crashed, largely as a result of the eradication of weeds from most agricultural crops. The Linnet nests in hedgerows, and in winter flocks, often with other finches, and sometimes moves into suburban areas.

Below: *The Linnet is a hedgerow bird par excellence. They often nest in gardens in rural areas, but are mostly likely to be found in waste ground in built-up areas.*

Breeding
Linnets build a cup nest in a hedge or bush or low vegetation. They lay 4–6 pale eggs spotted with reddish brown, which hatch after 10–14 days. The young fledge after 11–13 days. They lay 2–3 clutches.

Feeding
During the breeding season they are mostly insectivorous, but feed on seeds throughout the rest of the year. They do come to feeders, but generally in more rural areas.

Bullfinch *Pyrrhula pyrrhula*

Identification
A striking, large finch, up to 16 cm (6.5 in), the male is bright pink on the underside, with a jet-black cap and bill. The back is bluish grey, and the wings and tail are black. They have a white wing bar and a broad white rump, The female is similar, but has a buff-pink underside. Bullfinches are generally rather shy, and often seen in pairs. The call is a quiet, fluty whistle.

In the Garden
Regular visitors to gardens, particularly in areas near to woodlands or orchards. Like the majority of birds associated with farmland the Bullfinch has declined dramatically in the past quarter of a century.

Breeding
Builds a loose nest of roots and small twigs lined with moss and hair. It lays 3–6 eggs, which are sky-blue with a few black spots. The eggs are incubated for 12–14 days, and the young fledge after 15–17 days.

Feeding
Bullfinches feed on seeds, but also cause damage to fruit trees, feeding on grubs and buds.

Above: *The bright pink plumage of the male Bullfinch contrasts with the jet black on the upperparts. Although surprisingly widespread, they are often shy, hiding in shrubs and bushes.*

ground, and build a cup of grasses and moss lined with grass and hair. They lay 3–5 eggs which are white with a distinctive purple 'scribble'. They hatch after 11–14 days. The young leave the nest at about 14 days and are flying 2 days later.

Feeding
They feed on seeds during most of the year, but largely insects during the breeding season.

Below: *The Yellowhammer is comparatively rare in towns and suburban areas, but still reasonably abundant in rural areas, where it nests in hedgerows and similar habitats.*

Yellowhammer *Emberiza citrinella*

Identification
A large bunting, up to 16 cm (6.5 in), with a characteristic yellowish plumage. The male has a bright yellow head and throat, and a rich chestnut rump. The female is similar but duller. Both are quite heavily streaked with browns. The song is easily recognized and usually transcribed as 'a little bit of bread and no cheeeeze'.

In the Garden
No longer common in gardens, even in rural areas. As with most other farmland birds, numbers have declined dramatically, and appear to be continuing to do so. Yellowhammers form flocks in winter, often mixed with finches, and in hard weather may visit bird tables. They generally feed on the ground.

Breeding
They nest in hedgerows, usually on or close to the

FROGS AND TOADS

There are three species of frog and toad native to the British Isles but several others have been introduced in the past two centuries. The native species all migrate to ponds and lakes to lay their eggs, or spawn, in water. The tadpoles usually change into their adult form in late summer or early autumn, but occasionally they overwinter as tadpoles.

Above: Common Frogs are usually the commonest amphibians in suburban ponds. Some individuals will stay in the water all the year, but most move on land outside the breeding season.

Common Frog *Rana temporaria*

Identification
A smooth-skinned amphibian, which is extremely variable in colouring, but most often browns and yellowish greens, with black barring on the legs. It grows to about 10 cm (4 in). It is often easier to observe frogs in a pond using a powerful torch at night.

In the Garden
They occur in a very wide range of habitats over most of Europe and also in Ireland where they were introduced in the 20th century. They are usually found fairly close to water. However, terrestrial habitat in a garden is just as important as a pond. When stocking a pond, a small clump of spawn can be transferred from another pond, but this should always be in the near vicinity, and with the landowner's permission.

Breeding
Frogs come to ponds as early as December and January in the warmer parts of Britain and Europe, but mostly start to breed once frosts have stopped. During the breeding season the males develop black nuptial pads on the thumbs to assist grasping the females. The spawn is laid in large clumps. The froglets usually emerge in late summer, often during a rain shower and spend the next two or three years on land, in damp habitats, including lush grass.

Feeding
They feed on insects and other invertebrates.

Marsh Frog *Rana ridibunda*

There are several species of closely related marsh and pool frogs in continental Europe, some of which hybridize. They have also been moved around by humans and introduced in several places. The Marsh Frog was introduced into England in the 1920s and colonized Romney Marsh in Kent, but at the end of the 20th century it started to spread more widely and there is concern that it is displacing the Common Frog. More recently the American Bullfrog has been introduced and is spreading in England.

Below: The Marsh Frog was introduced into Kent and is now widespread. It can be recognized by its noisy croaking, and it often basks floating on the water, or close to water.

Common Toad *Bufo bufo*

Identification
A warty-skinned amphibian, generally various shades of brown or reddish brown. Males are smaller than females, the latter growing up to 10 cm (4 in) or more.

In the garden
This toad often moves a considerable distance from water outside the breeding season. Toads are common in gardens and long-lived. They are mostly nocturnal, spending the day under paving slabs, in woodpiles and similar situations. In summer, they can often be seen waiting for moths to fall beneath exterior floodlights.

Breeding
In spring, the males often wait for the females around ponds and attach themselves to a female to be carried along until she spawns. They lay their spawn in long strings, which are wrapped around aquatic vegetation.

Feeding
They feed on almost any invertebrates that are slow enough for them to catch.

He makes regular visits to water to keep the eggs moist and when they are developed, the tadpoles swim away.

Feeding
Like other toads, the Midwife Toad eats almost any small invertebrate it can catch.

Above: *The Common Toad is often described as the gardener's friend. It feeds extensively on invertebrates, particularly those which are pests in the garden.*

Below: *A male Midwife Toad carrying the string of eggs. They have to be regularly dampened and are finally taken to water when the tadpoles hatch.*

Midwife Toad *Ayletes obstetricans*

Identification
A small toad, usually less than 5 cm (2 in) long. It is strictly nocturnal, hiding in burrows and crevices by day. At night it has a ventriloquial call, similar to Scops Owl – a quiet, bell-like 'poo-poo-poo'. Its pupil is vertical – the Common Toad has a horizontal pupil.

In the Garden
Widespread in western Europe, it has been introduced into England and occurs in a small area of central England, where it is found in gardens.

Breeding
Unlike most amphibians the female does not lay eggs in water. Instead she lays strings of eggs which the male wraps around his hind legs and carries with him.

NEWTS AND SALAMANDERS

Newts are tailed amphibians, closely related to salamanders. Newts breed in water and the males develop distinctive breeding dress. Like frogs, newts need ponds to breed in and also suitable terrestrial habitats in which to spend the year outside the breeding season. When in the water they are usually easier to observe by searching with a torch at night. The larvae have feathery gills and the four legs develop simultaneously.

Crested Newt *Triturus cristatus*

Identification
The adults are large, up to 15 cm (6 in) long, with a rough, rather warty skin, black above, with an orange-yellow belly patterned with black. The sides are often stippled with silvery white and the males develop a spiky crest in the breeding season.

In the Garden
Widespread over much of northern Europe, but absent from Ireland. Outside the breeding season most likely to be found under paving stones, in wood or brick piles, usually fairly close to water. They can be found in their breeding ponds almost all the months of the year.

Breeding
They start breeding in early spring, when 200–400 eggs are laid singly, attached to aquatic vegetation. Only half the eggs develop, owing to a chromosomal abnormality.

Feeding
Tadpoles and frogspawn in the water, as well as a wide variety of invertebrates. On land, particularly after rain, they can often be seen at night lying in wait for slugs and other prey.

Below: *The Crested Newt is spectacular. During the breeding season it is best observed at night using a powerful torch.*

Above: *The male Common Newt has extensive crests during the breeding season. Once they have bred and left the water, the males appear very similar to the females.*

Smooth Newt *Triturus vulgaris*

Identification
Rarely more than 10 cm (4 in) long, the terrestrial form is rather lizard-like – brown above and with a black-spotted orange belly. But it is never as fast-moving as lizards, and the skin is smooth and velvety – never scaly and dry like that of a lizard. During the breeding season the male develops spectacular crests and colouring – frequently it is misidentified as a Crested Newt. The upperparts become greyer, with blackish spots.

In the Garden
Widespread over most of Europe, including Britain and Ireland. Generally the most common newt, which often colonizes garden ponds. Like all amphibians, it requires access to suitable terrestrial habitat as well as a pond. It is the most terrestrial of the newts.

Breeding
Breeds in spring, laying 200–300 eggs singly attached to the leaves of aquatic vegetation.

Feeding
It will eat almost any invertebrate it can catch. It also feeds on small tadpoles, frogspawn and fish fry.

Palmate Newt
Triturus helveticus

Identification
Slightly smaller than the Smooth Newt, growing to a maximum of 9 cm (3.5 in). Outside the breeding season it is difficult to distinguish from the Smooth Newt, but is most easily identified by the lack of spotting on the throat. During the breeding season, the male develops a slight, smooth crest on the tail and a black filament at the end of the tail. The hind feet are black and palmate.

In the Garden
Widespread in western Europe, but absent from Ireland. Often occurs in the same ponds as other newts, but where it overlaps with the Common Newt, tends to prefer more acid ponds.

Breeding
The Palmate Newt lays up to 460 eggs, attached singly to aquatic vegetation. When the newly metamorphosed newts emerge onto dry land they have an orange stripe down the middle of the back.

Feeding
Takes small invertebrates such as earthworms and slugs.

Above: *A male Palmate Newt clearly showing the palmated hind feet from which it takes its name.*

Below: *The Fire Salamander is confined to continental Europe and some Mediterranean islands. Its bright coloration is a warning to would-be predators that it has poisonous secretions from the large glands on the side of its head and other parts of the body.*

the female gives birth to a smaller number of fully metamorphosed young.

Feeding
Salamanders feed on invertebrates, normally during or after rain, and at night.

Fire Salamander *Salamandra salamandra*

Identification
Jet-black with bright yellow or orange blotches. It grows up to about 20 cm (8 in), including its tail. The amount of yellow varies considerably.

In the Garden
Widespread over most of western and central Europe in a range of habitats, but absent from the British Isles. Its typical habitat is forests.

Breeding
The female normally gives birth to well developed larvae, depositing up to 70 in clear, often running, water. The larvae usually overwinter in water. Sometimes

LIZARDS AND SNAKES

Lizards and snakes are reptiles and mostly found in the warmer parts of the world. Only four lizard species occur in northern Europe. Some lizards are legless or have reduced limbs, and there is considerable variation in their breeding biology. They are all sun-loving; to provide suitable habitat in a garden, it is important to make good places for them to bask.

Above: *The Common Lizard, like other reptiles, needs to spend much of the day basking in sunshine to maintain its body temperature. When disturbed it scuttles away into cover.*

Common Lizard *Lacerta vivipara*

Identification
A small brownish lizard, often with an olive iridescence. The underside is usually orange or reddish. It grows up to 17 cm (6.5 in), including a tail that is over half the total length.

In the Garden
Once common and widespread, it is very vulnerable to predation by cats and rats, and has declined dramatically in the past half century. If present, lizards can be encouraged by keeping a garden cat-free, and providing south-facing embankments and brush piles. Sheets of corrugated iron and stone piles are also useful.

Breeding
Common Lizards are live-bearing, retaining the eggs within the body, and giving birth to tiny, almost jet-black babies. Their dark colouring ensures maximum heat absorption.

Feeding
Almost any small invertebrates; also some fruit such as blackberries in autumn.

Wall Lizard *Podarcis muralis*

Identification
Similar to the Common Lizard, but slightly larger, with a total length of up to 21 cm (8.5 in), including a tail of up to 14 cm (5.5 in). It is slightly more slender and generally more olive in colour, although the colour is extremely variable.

In the Garden
Widespread in western Europe as far north as northern France, but absent from the British Isles. Along with several other closely related species, it was frequently imported into Britain and sold in petshops, and many attempts were made to introduce them. Most failed, but some colonies survived for several years.

Breeding
Wall Lizards lay up to 9 eggs in loamy soil.

Feeding
They eat small invertebrates, and also fruit in autumn.

Below: *Wall Lizards occur in a wide variety of habitats, and in southern Europe there is a considerable range of species.*

Above: In gardens, the Slow Worm is easily attracted to pieces of sheet metal, which warm up rapidly in the morning sun, and provide a home safe from most predators.

Slow Worm *Anguis fragilis*

Identification
A slender, legless lizard, with very fine scales, which give it a very smooth, shiny appearance. The colouring is variable, but generally bronze or pinkish. The females may have dark undersides; some have blue spotting on the sides. The tail is frequently broken, and scarcely regenerates. Slow Worms can grow to 50 cm (19.5 in), but are usually much smaller.

In the Garden
Widespread in northern Europe including England and Wales. In rural areas the Slow Worm is not uncommon in gardens, and churchyards, but is still often needlessly persecuted because of its resemblance to a snake. It can be encouraged by placing corrugated iron sheets around, and providing log and stone piles for it to use for shelter and for basking.

Breeding
Slow Worms retain the 6–12 eggs within the body, laying them at the point of hatching. The newborn young are bright copper above and jet-black below, with a thin black line down the back.

Feeding
They feed mostly on small slugs as well as earthworms and other similar soft-bodied invertebrates.

Grass Snake *Natrix natrix*

Identification
Grows up to 1.2 m (47 in), occasionally longer. The body colour is olive-green, with black barring and a bright yellow collar. The Adder is a much plumper, generally sandy, grey or brown snake, with a characteristic zig-zag pattern. It is poisonous, but rarely causes fatalities.

In the Garden
Widespread across most of Europe except the north. In more rural areas it can be a frequent visitor, feeding in ponds, and breeding in compost heaps. When handled Grass Snakes hiss, can feign death, and eject a pungent-smelling foul liquid from the cloaca. They can be encouraged by providing shelter, such as corrugated iron sheets, as well as manure heaps, and leaving compost heaps undisturbed.

Breeding
They lay up to 25 oval eggs, in a compost heap or manure heap; the eggs hatch after about 6–10 weeks.

Feeding
They feed exclusively on live prey, including frogs, toads and fish. They often swim, and can be seen basking at the water's edge, diving when disturbed.

Below: The Grass Snake is easily identified by its bright yellow collar and black barring. The loss of large muckheaps has reduced the Grass Snake's potential breeding sites.

HAWKMOTHS

Hawkmoths are among the largest moths and their caterpillars are often spectacular. They are mostly night-flying and can often be found around exterior lights. Many of the hawkmoths have a rather triangular shape, and like other moths they are distinguished from butterflies by the shape of their antennae. Similar to other nocturnal moths, hawkmoths can be attracted by sugaring.

Privet Hawkmoth *Sphinx ligustri*

Identification
The caterpillar grows to about 10 cm (4 in) long and is bright green, with 7 purplish-red and white diagonal stripes on each side, and a dark tail 'horn'.

In the Garden
One of the commonest hawkmoths within its range, it occurs widely in Europe, and in the southern half of Britain, but is absent from the north and Ireland. They are often the most familiar hawkmoths in suburban areas, because of the abundance of their food plants.

Breeding
It has a single brood each year, laying its eggs singly in June or July. The caterpillars pupate in late summer, burrowing deep in to the ground, and emerge the following summer. Sometimes the pupae spend two winters underground.

Feeding
The caterpillars feed on privet, and also lilac and ash.

Below: *A Privet Hawkmoth, seen here on the food plant to which it owes its name. Like other hawkmoths, the caterpillars of this species are large and spectacular.*

Above: *The Hummingbird Hawkmoth can be attracted to gardens by ensuring a supply of nectar-bearing shrubs.*

Hummingbird Hawkmoth *Macroglossum stellatarum*

Identification
A day-flying moth that is usually seen hovering in front of highly scented flowers such as jasmine and honeysuckle. It is about 2.5 cm (1 in) long, with a wingspan of 4.5 cm (1.75 in). As its name suggests it is remarkably like a hummingbird, with a very fast flight, pausing and hovering in front of flowers, and inserting its long tongue to extract nectar, before rapidly moving to the next flower. The Hummingbird Hawkmoth caterpillar is slender, with a short tail spike. It is bright green with two yellow stripes running down each side.

In the Garden
A common visitor to gardens, it will allow close approach.

Breeding
In Britain it is a migrant, arriving in spring and summer, and laying its eggs singly on food plants. The eggs hatch a week later, and the caterpillars pupate in cocoons on the ground, emerging after about a month. These moths do not normally survive the winter in Britain.

Feeding
The caterpillars feed on hedge bedstraw, lady's bedstraw and wild madder.

Broad-bordered Bee Hawkmoth
Hemaris fuciformis

Identification
The Bee Hawkmoth also occurs commonly in gardens, and this species has transparent bee-like wings, with a wingspan of 4.5 cm (1.75 in). The caterpillars are pale green with red-centred yellow spots on the sides, and a dark tail 'horn'.

In the Garden
A day-flying moth, occasionally seen in gardens, it can be attracted by planting its favoured food plant – honeysuckle.

Breeding
Broad-bordered Bee Hawkmoths have a single brood, laying their eggs singly on the underside leaves in May or June. The caterpillars pupate below ground, and emerge the following May.

Feeding
The caterpillars feed on honeysuckle.

Eyed Hawkmoth *Smerinthus ocellata*

Identification
At rest it is well camouflaged with a dead-leaf pattern, but each hind wing has a distinctive 'eye' on a pink background. The caterpillar is up to 8 cm (3.5 in) long and pale yellowish green with white (sometimes red-centred) spots on the side, pale diagonal stripes, and a green tail 'horn'.

In the Garden
They are widespread across Europe, including England and Wales, and more locally in Ireland.

Breeding
They have a single brood, laying their eggs singly on the underside of the leaves of the food plant. The caterpillars pupate in September in a cocoon just below the surface of the ground, and the adults emerge the following year, in May or June.

Above: *This photograph clearly shows how closely the Bee Hawkmoth resembles a Bee.*

Feeding
The caterpillars feed on sallows and willows (*Salix* spp.) as well as poplar, apple and some other species. The adult, in common with many other species of hawkmoth, feeds on nectar and can be attracted by sugaring a fence post. This is a mixture of syrup and beer.

Below: *Normally the 'eyes' on the Eyed Hawkmoth are concealed by the forewings, so that when exposed they startle potential predators.*

MOTHS

There are hundreds of species of moths. Most are nocturnal and many are extremely small and inconspicuous. However, among the many species that you may encounter in your garden, here are some of the more widespread and colourful.

Pussmoth *Cerura vinula*

Identification
The adult is white, with black markings and feathery antennae and a wingspan of 2.5 cm (1 in), but the caterpillar is spectacular. Growing up to 6.5 cm (2.5 in), it is very plump, with a tapering rear that ends in two long tail filaments. It is bright green with a red 'face'. When disturbed, the caterpillar has a threat display, rearing up and waving the tail. It can also spray an acid from behind its head.

In the Garden
It is a widespread species, found throughout most of Europe, including the British Isles.

Breeding
There is one brood a year and the eggs are laid in small clumps on the food plant in May or June. They pupate in

Above: *The dramatic caterpillar of the Pussmoth.*

Left: *The adult Pussmoth has a colouring designed to camouflage it on bark- and lichen-covered trees.*

September, making a cocoon out of silk and chewed bark, attached to the tree trunk.

Feeding
The caterpillars feed on willows and sallows (*Salix* spp.) and also poplars and aspens (*Populus* spp.).

Garden Tiger *Arctia caja*

Identification
The adult is an attractive brown and white when settled and in flight exposes a bright orange hind wing, with 6 jet-black spots. It has a wingspan of 4.5 cm (1.75 in).

In the Garden
A widespread and common species, likely to occur almost anywhere its food plants grow.

Breeding
There is a single brood which hatches in August. The caterpillars hibernate and emerge the following spring to continue growth. They pupate in summer in a cocoon in leaf litter, emerging in July and August.

Feeding
The caterpillars feed on a very wide range of both wild and cultivated garden plants, including trees and shrubs.

Below: *The Garden Tiger, like all other tiger moths, is brightly coloured and spotted – not striped as its name would suggest.*

Cinnabar Moth
Callimorpha jacobaeae

Identification
A day-flying moth, it has a black body, about 1.5 cm (0.5 in) long and bright red and black wings, with a wingspan of 3.5–4.5 cm (1.4–1.8 in). The caterpillars pupate in autumn and overwinter in the pupa, emerging in May. The caterpillars grow to 3 cm (1.5 in) and have a warning coloration of bright yellow and black bands as they are distasteful to most predators. They are gregarious and very conspicuous.

In the Garden
Often common and widespread wherever its food plant is found. It is often particularly abundant along roadsides and on railway embankments.

Breeding
A single brood is laid in large clumps on the underside of leaves in June. The caterpillars pupate in autumn, emerging in May or June the following year.

Feeding
Most commonly found on ragwort, but sometimes occurs on other related *Senecio* spp.

Above: *The Cinnabar Moth is one of the relatively few day-flying moths and is most likely to be seen on waste ground and similar habitats, as its caterpillars feed on ragwort, which is generally considered a weed.*

Below: *Nondescript and well camouflaged at rest, the Broad-bordered Yellow Underwing only shows its colour in flight.*

When they emerge from hibernation, they feed on the young growth of deciduous trees and shrubs.

Feeding
The caterpillars feed on hawthorn, primrose, dock, dead nettle, blackthorn, birch and several other common hedging and garden plants.

Broad-bordered Yellow Underwing
Noctua fimbriata

Identification
At rest it is not particularly striking, but when it flies, the brightly coloured hind wing is exposed, with contrasting orange and black. It has a wingspan of 4.5–5.5 cm (1.75–2.2 in). There are several closely related species with underwing colouring ranging from yellow through orange to red.

In the Garden
Widespread and common in gardens and often seen attracted to exterior lights.

Breeding
There is a single brood, the eggs being laid in late summer.

141

BUTTERFLIES

With their large bright wings and conspicuous day-flying habits, butterflies are probably the most popular insects. On the wing during the spring and summer months, several species are visitors to gardens where they will feed on the nectar of vivid flower heads and lay their eggs on a variety of food plants.

Above: The Small Tortoiseshell is one of the most common and widespread butterflies, feeding on the nectar of flowers, and often found hibernating in attics or sheds in winter.

Small Tortoiseshell *Aglais urticae*

Identification
The adults are among our most familiar and colourful butterflies with a wingspan of 5–5.5 cm (19.5–2.2 in). The caterpillars are black with tiny white spots and a broken band of yellowish down each side. There are spines on the back and they grow to just over 2 cm (0.75 in).

In the Garden
A widespread and common species often seen in gardens. Easily attracted to feed on flowering shrubs, particularly buddleia. The caterpillars are very similar to those of Red Admiral and Peacock, which are also common on nettles.

Breeding
They have 2 broods, the first in early summer. The second brood hibernates as adults, which lay eggs when they emerge in spring. The caterpillars pupate about a month after hatching and the pupae are suspended from the stems of nettles.

Feeding
The caterpillars feed on stinging nettles. They are gregarious, living under a web.

Peacock *Inachis io*

Identification
A large, unmistakable butterfly, with prominent 'eyes' on each wing, it has a wingspan of 6.3–6.9 cm (2.5–2.7 in). The caterpillars are black, with spines on the back.

In the Garden
One of the commonest and most widespread butterflies in Europe, including the British Isles. Attracted to many blossoms, but particularly buddleia.

Breeding
One brood a year, the eggs are laid singly, with the caterpillars living in colonies under a web. The pupae are suspended from the stems and the butterflies emerge in late summer, but do not mate and lay eggs until they emerge after hibernation the following year.

Feeding
The caterpillars feed on stinging nettles.

Left: The Peacock is one of the most spectacular of several species of butterflies and moths that have 'eyes' on their wings, which are used to fool would-be predators.

Red Admiral *Vanessa atalanta*

Identification
A striking butterfly, mostly dark brown and black, with prominent red bands on the fore wing, it has a wingspan of 7 cm (2.75 in). The caterpillars are black with spines on the back and often very similar to those of the Peacock and Small Tortoiseshell, but the colouring is variable.

In the Garden
One of the commonest and most abundant butterflies, it is a migrant from southern Europe and does not always survive hibernation. It is easily attracted to flowers, particularly buddleia.

Breeding
There are 1 or 2 broods. The eggs are laid singly on the upper side of leaves and the caterpillars live in curled leaves, where they also pupate, emerging 2–3 weeks later.

Feeding
Like the Peacock and Small Tortoiseshell, its caterpillar is commonly found on stinging nettles, but it also feeds on hops and other species.

Above: There is an annual influx of Red Admirals, which breed in Europe, but rarely survive the winters.

Large White *Pieris brassicae*

Identification
Creamy white, with three large, black spots and tips to the fore wings and a black spot at the top of the hind wing. The Large White has a wingspan of 7 cm (2.75 in). The caterpillars are fairly slender, up to 4 cm (1.5 in) long, and heavily spotted with yellow, black and green. The bright colouring warns predators that they are distasteful.

In the Garden
Easily attracted by planting brassica, such as cabbage, broccoli and sprouts. One of the commonest butterflies, it often reaches pest proportions if the caterpillars are not removed from crops. Along with the closely related Small White, it is often referred to as the 'Cabbage White' by gardeners. The caterpillar of the Small White is smooth, bright green with yellow spots on the sides. There are several other less common species of 'White' butterflies, which do not normally feed on brassica (cabbage family).

Breeding
They have two generations a year, the eggs being laid in clumps on leaves in May and July. The caterpillars are gregarious and have a noxious smell.

Feeding
Although they are commonest on cabbages and, as most gardeners know, can become a serious pest, they also feed on nasturtium and several other plants, both cultivated and wild.

Below: The Large White Butterfly is one of several species referred to by most gardeners simply as the Cabbage White.

Above: *The Brimstone Butterfly takes its name from its sulphurous yellow colouring.*

Brimstone *Gonepteryx rhamni*

Identification
The adults are unmistakable, a pale lemon yellow, with small orange spots in the centre of each wing. They have a wingspan of 6 cm (2.4 in). The caterpillars are a peacock green above, with a white stripe down the sides and green on the underside. They grow to 33 mm (1.3 in) long.

In the Garden
A common and widespread species except in the north. It occurs mostly in chalky and limestone areas and can be attracted to gardens by planting their food plants.

Breeding
They have a single brood and the eggs are laid singly on the underside of leaves in May. The pupae are attached to the stems of the food plant and the butterflies emerge a fortnight later. After hibernation, they mate and lay eggs the following year.

Feeding
The caterpillars feed almost exclusively on buckthorn and alder buckthorn.

Common Blue *Polyommatus icarus*

Identification
The Common Blue is one of a large group of often very similar small butterflies. It is pale blue, with dark edges to the wings and a wingspan of 3.5 cm (1.4 in). The caterpillar is small and plump, tapering at the head and tail. It is green with longitudinal stripes.

In the Garden
A butterfly of downland and meadows, the Common Blue can be attracted to gardens by allowing lawns to become diversified.

Breeding
Double-brooded with the first eggs laid singly on the upper surfaces of leaves in early summer. They pupate at the base of the food plant and the second generation overwinters as caterpillars, emerging the following spring to complete the life-cycle.

Feeding
The caterpillars of the Common Blue Butterfly feed on clovers, bird's-foot trefoil, rest-harrow and other related plants.

Below: *The Common Blue is one of the most widespread of a very large group of closely related butterflies. It is sun-loving, and likes areas of long grass in the garden.*

Above: *The male Gatekeeper seen here is significantly smaller than the female and has a richer, more intense colouring. The similar Meadow Brown is larger and duller.*

Gatekeeper *Pyronia tithonus*

Identification

A small orange-brown butterfly, with white-centred black spots at the front of each of the fore wings, with a wingspan of 4–4.7 cm (1.5–1.85 in). Rather like a smaller, more brightly coloured Meadow Brown. The small caterpillar is up to 2.3 cm (1 in), pale brownish-white and tapering at the head and tail.

In the Garden

A common butterfly found in hedges and woodland edges, it can be attracted to gardens by leaving grass to grow.

Breeding

A single brood, the eggs are laid singly on grass stems in July and August and the caterpillars hibernate in October, emerging in spring and pupating in June.

Feeding

The caterpillars feed on grasses.

Small Copper *Lycaena phlaeas*

Identification

A very small, brightly copper-brown butterfly with dark spotting, it has a wingspan of 3.5 cm (1.4 in). The caterpillar is a tiny oval, tapering at both ends, green with a longitudinal, pinkish-purple stripe each side and down the centre of the back.

In the Garden

A widespread and often common butterfly over most of Europe. It is common in pastures and other open grassland habitats, and can be attracted to gardens by allowing its foodplants to grow.

Breeding

A prolific species, it has 2 or 3 generations a year. The eggs are laid singly at the base of leaves and the caterpillars are usually found on the underside of the leaves. They overwinter as caterpillars, pupating in the spring in pupae attached to the underside of leaves or stems.

Feeding

The caterpillars feed on docks and sorrel (*Rumex* spp.). There are attractive garden varieties of the former and the latter can be grown as a culinary herb.

Below: *The Small Copper is bright orange. Despite superficial differences it is related to the 'Blue' butterflies. In fact, the underside of the wings of both groups are often very similar.*

GRASSHOPPERS AND WEEVILS

Grasshoppers and their close relatives the crickets seem to have declined in many areas. Grasshoppers are unusual in that many species communicate with stridulating 'songs' produced by rubbing the legs against the body. They also have 'ears' on the side of the body. Grasshoppers start life as nymphs, passing through several stages before reaching maturity without pupating. Weevils are superficially similar to beetles, with hard elytra (wing cases), but they have a distinctive 'trunk'.

Above: *The Oak Bush Cricket has the typical long antennae of the bush crickets. They are also known as Long-horned Grasshoppers.*

Oak Bush Cricket
Meconema thalassinum

Identification
It is 1.2-1.5 cm (0.5 in) long, with very long slender antennae, and the female has a 9 mm (0.3 in) long ovipositor. They are bright green, with a brown stripe down the centre of the back.

In the Garden
Widespread in continental Europe, it also occurs in southern England. These crickets are nocturnal, and the males drum on leaves with their hind feet, producing a sound that carries for several metres. They occur in oak, apples and many other deciduous trees and bushes, and are often found around lights and windows at night.

Breeding
Eggs are laid in vegetation.

Feeding
Mostly on oak, but also lime trees.

Common Field Grasshopper
Chorthippus brunneus

Identification
A medium-sized grasshopper, up to 1.8 cm (0.7 in) long, greyish brown, green or purplish black, and the male has a reddish tip to the abdomen. The male's call is 6–10 short chirps.

In the Garden
Increasingly rare, but still found in many parks, commons and larger gardens. The main cause of decline is probably the lack of long grass, and they can be encouraged by leaving areas of unmown

Below: *The Common Field Grasshopper is not so common as formerly. It is likely that mechanical lawnmowers destroy large numbers of insects such as grasshoppers.*

Above: A Common Field Grasshopper, which is distinguished from bush crickets, or Long-horned Grasshoppers, by its much shorter antennae.

grass. They are usually seen between July and October. Modern high-speed mowers kill them easily and short grass makes them vulnerable to predators.

Breeding
The eggs are laid in autumn and the nymphs emerge in the spring.

Feeding
It feeds mostly on grasses.

Vine weevil
Otiorhynchus sulcatus

Identification
One of the largest weevils in the region, growing up to 1.2 cm (0.5 in) long. The Vine Weevil is black with long antennae, which are 'elbowed' and has a characteristic 'trunk'. The grubs are large, white and legless. Numerous other weevils are also very common in stored foods, as well as in the garden.

In the Garden
The weevil's larvae cause considerable damage to a wide range of plants, not just vines, but also auriculas, fuchsias and other popular garden varieties. The Vine Weevil's success as a pest is partly due to its diverse taste. They feed on the roots of just about anything, even poisonous plants such as taxus. The Vine Weevil is likely to be encountered in greenhouses where they are safe from their predators. The weevil can be controlled using traps or biological controls. Adults are strictly nocturnal.

Breeding
They are parthenogenetic, that is female only, and they can lay up to 1,000 eggs over the course of the summer.

Feeding
The grubs feed on roots, often causing considerable damage to cultivated plants. They can be destroyed by using biological controls such as nematodes.

Below: An adult Vine Weevil. It is almost exclusively nocturnal and feeds on leaves which does relatively little harm. The grubs, however, can cause serious damage.

BEETLES

Beetles make up the largest group of insects and there are numerous species that occur in gardens. They are easily recognized as a group, having hard front wings (elytra), which usually cover the abdomen. Beetles start life as grubs and pupate, sometimes taking several years to reach maturity.

Stag Beetle *Lucanus cervus*

Identification
A very large beetle of up to 2.5-7.5 cm (1–3 in). The males are larger than females and have large jaws that look like antlers. They have dark brown wing cases, with the head, jaws and legs black.

In the Garden
Once widespread and common over much of the region, their range includes southern England, but they have declined markedly, owing to loss of habitat. They can be encouraged by providing rotting logs and leaving dead trees standing.

Breeding
Stag Beetles lay their eggs in rotting wood and the grubs are whitish.

Feeding
The adults feed on oozing sap from trees and the grubs on rotting wood, particularly oak.

Above: *Burying Beetles perform a useful function in the garden by clearing away any small birds and mammals and burying them for their grubs to feed on.*

Burying Beetle *Nicrophorus vespillo*

Identification
The Burying Beetle is a medium-sized beetle, about 2 cm (0.8 in) long, mostly black with two broad orange-red bands across the wing cases. The antennae end in round clubs. There are several closely related, similar species.

In the Garden
One of the true burying beetles, it is attracted to corpses by their smell and excavates a hole beneath the body, often working in pairs, then dragging the corpse underground. Adults are sometimes attracted to lights at night.

Breeding
The female lays eggs on or close to the corpse of a mouse or bird.

Feeding
The adults and grubs feed on carrion and also on other insects attracted to the carrion.

Below: *The male Stag Beetle, showing the massive 'antlers' from which the species takes its name. The clearance of old trees has led to its decline in suburban areas.*

7-Spot Ladybird
Coccinella 7-punctata

Identification
The 7-spot is bright orange-red, with three spots on each of the wing cases and one spread across both. There are many other species, including 2-spot, 10-spot and 24-spot, which are also orange, as well as 14- and 22-spot, which are yellow with black spots.

In the Garden
Ladybirds are among the most familiar, most distinctive and most popular garden insects. In some years huge migrations take place.

Breeding
They lay clusters of 10–50 eggs in aphid colonies. The eggs hatch in 3–5 days and pupate 2–3 weeks later. There are up to 6 generations a year.

Feeding
Both adults and larvae feed on aphids.

Above: *The 7-spot Ladybird is one of the commonest and most widespread species. Large numbers hibernate and gardeners can help by providing suitable sites.*

Below: *The Devil's Coach Horse is unusual in that the adult looks very similar to a larval form; this is because of its tiny wing cases.*

Devil's Coach Horse *Staphylinus olens*

Identification
A flightless rove beetle, they are terrestrial and are long and narrrow in shape with short wing cases, lacking wings. It is about 30 mm (1.2 in) long, black and covered with fine hairs. When disturbed, it raises its tail and opens its jaws.

In the Garden
Widespread in hedgerows, woodland and in gardens and outhouses, where it usually hides among logs, under paving or stones and in other damp places.

Breeding
The female lays eggs on leaf piles and the grubs are a whitish grey.

Feeding
A nocturnal predator, feeding on slugs, snails and other small invertebrates.

DAMSELFLIES AND DRAGONFLIES

Dragonflies and damselflies are long-bodied insects, with very large eyes and two pairs of stiff, transparent wings. Closely related and similar species are usually identified by details in the venation of the wings. In flight the wings make a buzz or a rustling noise and they are very fast-flying. Their excellent eyesight enables them to prey on flying insects, which they scoop up using their bristly legs as a basket and then settle on a perch to eat. There are around 100 species in Europe. The eggs are laid in water or on aquatic vegetation and hatch into nymphs. These are aquatic and take between 1 and 5 years to mature, before climbing out of the water for the final moult into an adult.

Above: *The Large Red Damselfly is one of the first to appear in spring, often seen flying as early as March.*

Below: *A male Common Blue Damselfly. The female is darker and the blue areas are replaced with dull green. They are often one of the first species to colonize new ponds.*

Large Red Damselfly
Pyrrhosoma nymphula

Identification
A large slender-bodied damselfly with a bright red abdomen, black legs and red stripes on the thorax. It is 4 cm (1.57 in) long with a wingspan of 5 cm (2 in).

In the Garden
A common and widespread species, mostly found near slow-moving streams and rivers, as well as ponds, lakes and peat bogs.

Breeding
Breeds in slow-moving streams and still waters.

Feeding
The nymphs prey on aquatic animals, the adults on flying insects.

Common Blue Damselfly
Enallagma cyathigerum

Identification
A slender species, with a pale blue abdomen and a blue-striped thorax. There are several very similar and closely related species, but this is the most often encountered. It has a body length of about 3.2 cm (1.3 in) and a wingspan of up to 4.2 cm (1.7 in).

In the Garden
Common and widespread and is seen May to September.

Breeding
Breeds in ponds and lakes and other stillwaters.

Feeding
Nymphs prey on aquatic animals, the adults on insects.

Southern Hawker *Aeshna cyanea*

Identification
It is large, growing to about 6 cm (2.25 in) long, with a wingspan of 8.5 cm (3.3 in). The abdomen is banded black and greenish blue and there are green-blue stripes on the thorax. The sexes are similar.

In the Garden
One of the commonest and most widespread of the Hawkers, it can often be found a considerable distance from water, hunting along hedgerows and in woodland.

Breeding
Breeds in large ponds and lakes.

Feeding
The nymphs prey on aquatic animals, the adults on flying insects.

Darter *Libellula quadrimaculata*

Identification
Large, but short-bodied compared with hawkers and other dragonflies. The body is brown and 3 cm (1.2 in) long. There are two spots on each wing and a pale brown patch at the base of each hind wing. It has a wingspan of 4 cm (1.6 in).

Above: *A Southern Hawker that has just emerged from its nymph stage. It takes several hours for its wings to dry in the sun before it can fly.*

In the Garden
A widespread and often common species, particularly near larger ponds and lakes. They migrate in late summer, often in swarms.

Breeding
They breed in bogs, marshes and other stillwaters.

Feeding
The nymphs prey on aquatic animals and the adults on flying insects.

Right: *The Darter also known as the Four-spotted Chaser is a large dragonfly that often breeds in relatively small ponds. The adults are very territorial and aggressive.*

BEES, WASPS AND ANTS

Bees and wasps together with ants and sawflies belong to the order Hymenoptera, which contains well over 100,000 species worldwide. They show huge variation in shape, size, breeding biology and behaviour. Some species are highly colonial, some have venomous stings, some are parasitic and others almost microscopic. Many are persecuted, particularly those with stings, yet they can be very important parts of an ecosystem.

Garden Bumble Bee *Bombus hortorum*

Identification
A relatively large bumble bee, growing to about 2 cm (0.8 in) long, the thorax is black and yellow and the abdomen black and whitish; both abdomen and thorax are furry. Identification is very difficult as there is wide variation, and is further complicated by cuckoo bees, which parasitize nests of the Garden Bumble Bee.

In the Garden
One of many species that are common throughout Europe, this is particularly common in gardens. It nests below the ground, often in a mouse hole, and readily adapts to artificial nest boxes. The nest is made of grasses and moss, with wax cells in it. The ideal site for a nest box is in a sunny south-facing bank.

Breeding
Forms small annual colonies. The early spring workers are small, and males only appear in late summer. The mated females hibernate, to form new colonies the following spring.

Feeding
They feed almost exclusively on pollen and nectar.

Honey Bee *Apis mellifera*

Identification
A rather nondescript, brownish bee, some strains are almost black. Workers are 1.5 cm (0.6 in) long.

In the Garden
Originally domesticated in Asia, the Honey Bee is now widespread in Europe and all other parts of the world, and it often occurs in the wild. It is colonial, and in hives there can be as many as 50,000 workers. Wild colonies are usually in hollow trees, but can also be in roofs and outbuildings. They are important pollinators for fruit trees and other crops.

Breeding
Each colony contains a single egg-laying queen. When the hive becomes overcrowded, a new queen is reared, and she will fly off with part of the colony to start a fresh colony.

Feeding
Exclusively on nectar and pollen, making honey in order to store a food supply.

Above: *A Garden Bumble Bee, showing the thickly 'furred' body characteristic of most bumble bees.*

Left: *A Honey Bee feeding on Ivy flowers. Honey Bees are one of the very few domesticated insects, but in recent years disease has adversely affected them, and wiped out many feral colonies.*

Above: *A close-up of the head of a Common Wasp, showing the powerful jaws, which are used to chop woody vegetation with which they make the paper for their nests.*

Common Wasp *Vespula vulgaris*

Identification
The Common Wasp has a characteristic black and yellow abdomen and is 1.5 cm (0.6 in) long. There are several other closely related species found in Britain and Europe, but they can only be readily identified with close examination. Cuckoo Wasps lay their eggs in the nests of other colonial wasps.

In the Garden
The most common and widespread species of wasp. It builds a large colonial nest from wood which it chews to a paper. The nests are usually built in a tree hollow, or often in outbuildings or attics.

Breeding
The female workers maintain the colony throughout the summer, and at the end of the season a few males appear, which mate. Only mated females survive the winter. The following spring, these mated females (queens) form new colonies.

Feeding
The adults feed on nectar, but the grubs are fed on insects that the workers catch. They are important predators in the garden ecosystem.

Red Ant *Myrmica rufa*

Identification
Colonial insects, throughout most of the year only the workers are seen. They are 4–5 cm (0.2 in) long, and chestnut-brown. In late summer winged males and queens emerge, and they are half as big again as the workers.

In the Garden
Common and widespread. Colonies are often found under stones, paving slabs, and the like. The workers have a sting. The eggs are often sought after by other animals.

Breeding
Each colony contains one or more queens, which are essentially egg-laying machines, and the several hundred workers tend the eggs and young. The winged males and queens emerge, mate and then the queens shed their wings.

Feeding
They are omnivorous.

Below: *A colony of Red Ants exposed by lifting a paving slab. Although disliked by many gardeners, ants play an important part in any wildlife garden, and they are an important food for several species. Green Woodpeckers, in particular, are very partial to ants.*

OTHER INVERTEBRATES

Even in a city garden there will generally be a wide range of invertebrates, many of them very small indeed, creating a mini-ecosystem. In addition to the vast array of insects, there are earthworms, nematodes, myriapods (millipedes and centipedes), arachnids (harvestmen, spiders and mites), molluscs (slugs and snails), crustaceans (woodlice), all of which are often abundant, but not all are detrimental to the garden. Worms may make unsightly 'casts' on a manicured lawn, but they are providing vital aeration to the soil. While some slugs and snails eat seedlings and vegetables, others do a lot of good, cleaning up dead and decaying vegetation. It is important to know which species are harmful and which are beneficial – the indiscriminate use of pesticides can cause as much harm as good, since it can easily wipe out species that are keeping pests under control.

Earthworm *Lumbricus terrestris*

Identification
The Earthworm grows up to 30 cm (12 in) long, and has a characteristic segmented body of about 150 segments. Their colouring is variable but it is usually pinkish brown with a violet tinge. There are several other closely related species also found in gardens throughout northern Europe.

In the Garden
Earthworms live in topsoil, emerging at night, particularly after rain, to drag dead leaves and other vegetation into their burrows to eat. When surfacing they keep their tail well anchored in their burrow. Earthworms are a very important food for many other animals. In very cold weather they become dormant and in hot, dry weather they burrow deeply and become dormant.

Below: *An earthworm on the surface. Earthworms normally only come to the surface of the soil to mate – being hermaphrodite, they can mate with the first worm that comes along.*

Breeding
The Earthworm is a hermaphrodite. A pair will mate with each partner laying eggs.

Feeding
Earthworms feed on dead vegetation.

Garden Spider *Araneus diadematus*

Identification
Grows up to 1.3 cm (0.5 in) long. The males are smaller than females. It is usually brownish, yellowish greenish to dark brown and has a whitish irregular cross on the back.

In the Garden
The Garden Spider is one of the most widespread and common spiders. It builds an orb web in hedges and among herbaceous borders. It is preyed on by birds and other wildlife.

Below: *The Garden Spider is one of many orb web building species. Not all spiders build webs and the web designs vary from species to species.*

Breeding
The female lays her eggs in a silken sac and the young overwinter as eggs, hatching the following spring.

Feeding
It feeds on flies (*Diptera*) and flying insects which it catches in its web.

Zebra Spider *Salticus scenicus*

Identification
A small, 5-7 mm (0.2 in) jumping spider, rather variable, but generally black and white striped. It has two large eyes and the male has large fangs. It is diurnal.

In the Garden
A common species in gardens and not likely to be confused with any other. It is often found on walls and

fences and its pattern camouflages it against lichens.

Breeding
The female lays her eggs in a silken sac and the young overwinter as eggs, hatching the following spring.

Feeding
It stalks its prey.

White-lipped Banded Snail
Cepaea hortensis

Identification
A medium-sized snail, with a shell 2 cm (0.8 in) in diameter. The shell is usually yellow or yellowish-white with dark brown or black bands, but very variable. It is almost identical to the closely related Brown-lipped Banded Snail (*Cepaea nemoralis*).

In the Garden
Common, nocturnal and often seen after rain. During the day these species are well camouflaged among grassy stems. Song Thrushes often eat them and the remains of the shells surround the thrush's anvil.

Breeding
It lays clusters of eggs in the soil.

Feeding
It feeds on grass, lettuce and other tender plants.

Large Black Slug *Arion ater*

Identification
Large, up to 20 cm (8 in) long, but not always black. It can be chestnut, orange, grey, whitish, but also jet-black.

In the Garden
A common and widespread species, most often seen at night after rain. Comes on to lawns, often in some numbers, to feed on grass clippings.

Breeding
Lays clusters of pearly white eggs, of about 5 mm (0.2 in) in diameter, often in compost heaps.

Feeding
It is omnivorous, feeding on dead vegetation, dung and carrion and is therefore not a pest in the garden.

Above: *The Zebra Spider clearly shows how it got its name. They do not build webs, but hunt their prey using their excellent eyesight.*

Above: *The White-lipped Banded Snail which although very distinctively patterned is actually very well camouflaged when feeding among grass stems.*

Above: *A Large Black Slug living up to its name. Despite the prejudice of most gardeners, many species of slug play an important role in the ecology of the garden.*

USEFUL ADDRESSES AND WEBSITES

General

The Wildlife Trusts
The Kiln
Waterside
Mather Road, Newark
Nottinghamshire NG24 1WT
Tel: 0870 0367711
www.wildlifetrusts.org

Founded by Lord Rothschild in 1912, The Wildlife Trusts network covers the whole of the UK and the British Isles. They now have more than 2,500 nature reserves, most of which are free to enter. They also undertake lots of activities with local communities and schools on how to attract wildlife to your garden.

British Ecological Society (BES)
www.britishecologicalsociety.org

For the more technically minded, the BES publishes a range of important journals.

Linnean Society of London
Burlington House, Piccadilly,
London W1J 0BF
Tel: 020 7434 4479
www.linnean.org

For the serious naturalist, Fellows of the Linnean Society can use their splendid library facilities and receive their journals.

Royal Society for the Prevention of Cruelty to Animals (RSPCA)
Wilberforce Way
Southwater
Horsham
West Sussex RH13 9RS
Tel: 0870 333 5999
www.rspca.org.uk

Provides a valuable service, offering help and advice about the care of animals in distress or other unfamiliar situations.

Societies and Museums
Most counties have a natural history society, and there are often natural history societies and bird clubs covering even smaller areas. These are mostly devoted to recording the wildlife, and they often organize field excursions for members and work very closely with local Wildlife Trusts.

Most counties have a museum, usually with collections of local natural history, and they can also direct you to local natural history societies.

Birds

Royal Society for the Protection of Birds (RSPB)
The Lodge
Sandy
Bedfordshire SG19 2DL
Tel: 01767 680551
www.rspb.org.uk

The leading bird organization in the UK with over 1 million members. It has a network of reserves, most of which are open to members and the public.

British Trust for Ornithology (BTO)
The Nunnery
Thetford
Norfolk IP24 2PU
Tel: 01842 750050
www.bto.org

The leading scientific research organization for birds – join to become involved in surveys.

The Wildfowl & Wetlands Trust (WWT)
Slimbridge
Gloucestershire GL2 7BT
Tel: (01453) 891900 press 9 for a list of options
www.wwt.org.uk

Founded by Sir Peter Scott, its original remit has been expanded, and their nature reserves are well worth a visit. They now have a network of wetland reserves, including the centres at Slimbridge, and Barn Elms, London.

Mammals

Mammal Society
The Mammal Society,
2B Inworth Street
London SW11 3EP
Tel: 020 7350 2200
www.abdn.ac.uk/mammal

Covering all mammals, the society has organized many surveys including garden mammals.

The Bat Conservation Trust
15 Cloisters House
8 Battersea Park Road
London SW8 4BG
Tel: 020 7627 2629
www.bats.org.uk

The BCT has a network of local groups, and encourages active participation by its members.

Reptiles and Amphibians

Froglife
Mansion House
27-28 Market Place, Halesworth
Suffolk IP19 8AY
Tel: 01986 873733
www.froglife.org

Concerned with all amphibians and reptiles – not just frogs.

Insects and Invertebrates

Butterfly Conservation
Manor Yard
East Lulworth, Wareham
Dorset BH20 5QP
Telephone: 0870 7744309
www.butterfly-conservation.org

The leading organization concerned with butterflies, it has an excellent website. There are also specialist societies interested in dragonflies, spiders, molluscs and other invertebrates. These can easily be located on the internet, or through one of the other societies listed above.

Wildflowers

Plantlife
21 Elizabeth Street
London SW1W 9RP
Tel: 020 7808 0100
www.plantlife.org.uk
Plantlife campaigns for plant conservation and habitats.

Supplies

BIRDS

Haith's
J. E. Haith Ltd
65 Park Street, Cleethorpes
North East Lincolnshire DN35 7NF
Tel: 0800 298 7054
www.haiths.com

A unique partnership has been formed between The Wildlife Trusts and J. E. Haith birdfood suppliers to create the Bill Oddie Natural Choice range of birdfoods. For every birdfood purchase The Wildlife Trusts receives 2.5% to support their vital work.

Jacobi Jayne & Company
Maypole
Hoath
Canterbury CT3 4LW
Tel: 01227 714314
www.birdcare.com/jacobijayne

There are numerous suppliers of birdfood, nest boxes and other supplies, and it is now a multi-million pound industry. Jacobi Jayne are manufacturers and distributors of a wide range of very high quality supplies and most of the nest boxes and feeders shown in this book were supplied by them. While some of the boxes are relatively expensive, it should be borne in mind that they are made of 'woodcrete', which is extremely durable, and will outlast most other materials by many years. The website also includes Chris Mead's *The State of the Nation's Birds*, plus many other useful links.

For the DIY enthusiast, there are many guides to making nest boxes and feeding tables, and some very useful specialist designs can be found on the internet.

There are also several books with designs for more unusual nest boxes. Some are fairly outrageous, so always make sure they are practical as well as interesting or amusing. *The Bird Feeder Book* by Thom Boswell (see page 158) has some extremely amusing examples of feeders and nest boxes.

WILDFLOWER SEEDS

Many seed companies now sell wildflowers, but do ensure they are from the right area.

Suttons Seeds
Woodview Road
Paignton
Devon TQ4 7NG
Tel: 01803 696400
www.suttons-seeds.co.uk

The Wildlife Trusts and Sutton Seeds have teamed up to produce an excellent range of wildflower seeds – all from known UK provenance – that will attract wildlife to your garden.

Landlife Wildflowers Limited
National Wildflower Centre
Court Hey Park
Liverpool L16 3NA
Tel: 0151 737 1819
www.wildflower.org.uk

Websites

These are just a few leads to sites not already listed.

www.birdsofbritain.co.uk
A particularly useful site for beginners. It also includes an accommodation guide for anyone wishing to visit nature reserves throughout Britain.

www.fatbirder.com
The most comprehensive bird site.

www.birdcare.com
A very useful site run by Jacobi Jayne & Company.

www.nhm.ac.uk/science/projects/fff/
The Postcode Plants Database. By typing in your postcode you can download a list of all the plant species known to be native to the area.

www.nhm.ac.uk
The Natural History Museum's very comprehensive website; it will allow access to practically anything to do with wildlife and natural history.

biome.ac.uk/biome.html
A good portal to a wide range of natural history topics.

www.wildlife-gardening.co.uk
A website run by Jenny Steele who has also written extensively on wildlife gardening.

www.soilassociation.org
This is the leading organic website.

www.expertgardener.com
Most gardening magazines now have regular features on wildlife. This site gives an entry point to many other useful sites.

www.permaculture.co.uk
Permaculture is a particularly wildlife-friendly approach and this site provides a wealth of information.

Help protect the UK's wildlife by joining The Wildlife Trusts on 0870 0367711 or online at www.wildlifetrusts.org

FURTHER READING

General

Anon, *Wildlife on your Doorstep: The Living Countryside*; Reader's Digest, London, 1987

Burton, J. A. *Nature in the City*; Danbury Press, London, 1976

Mead, C. *The State of the Nation's Birds*; Whittet Books, Stowmarket, 2000

Identifying Wildlife

Burton, J. A. *Field Guide to the Mammals of Britain & Europe*; Kingfisher Books, London, 2002

Carter, D.J. & Hargreaves, B *Collins Guide to the Caterpillars of Britain & Europe*; HarperCollins, London, 1994

Chinery, M. *Collins Guide to the Insects of Britain & Western Europe*; (2nd reprint), HarperCollins, London, 1993

Chinery, M. *Collins Nature Guides: Garden Wildlife of Britain & Europe*; HarperCollins, London, 1997

Hammond, N. *The Wildlife Trusts Handbook of Garden Wildlife*; New Holland Publishers, London, 2002

Harrison, C. *Collins Field Guide: Bird Nests, Eggs and Nestlings of Britain & Europe*; HarperCollins, London, 1998

Mullarney, K. et al. *Collins Bird Guide*; HarperCollins, London, 2001

Sample, G. *Collins Field Guide to the Bird Songs and Calls of Britain & Northern Europe*; HarperCollins, London, 1996

Gardening

Andrews, J. *The Country Diary Book of Creating a Wild Flower Garden*; Webb & Bower, Exeter, 1986

Bardsley, S. *The Wildlife Pond Handbook*; New Holland Publishers, London, 2003

Barrett, R. *The Pet Friendly Garden*; Pan, London, 2000

Beddard, R. *The Garden Bird Year*; New Holland Publishers, London, 2001

Rothschild, M. & Farrell, C. *The Butterfly Gardener*; Michael Joseph, London, 1983

Verner, Y. *Creating a Flower Meadow*; Green Earth Books, Totnes, 1998

Bird and Wildlife Feeding

Boswell, T. *The Bird Feeder Book*; Sterling, 1993

Burton, R. *Birdfeeder Handbook*; Dorling Kindersley, London, 1990

Golley, M., Moss, S. *The Complete Garden Bird Book*; New Holland Publishers, London, 2001

Moss, S. *Attracting Birds to Your Garden*; New Holland Publishers, London, 1998

Packham, C. *Chris Packham's Back Garden Nature Reserve*; New Holland, London, 2001

Soper, T. *The Bird Table Book*; David & Charles, Dawlish, 1965

Magazines

Most of the organizations listed on page 157 produce newsletters, and in some cases more technical journals as well. There are surprisingly few magazines available from bookstalls and newsagents.

BBC Wildlife
BBC Wildlife is a popular monthly magazine, which usually has several articles on British Wildlife. It is also available by subscription from:
BBC Wildlife Subscriptions
PO Box 279
Sittingbourne, Kent ME9 8DF
Tel: 01795 414718

British Wildlife
An excellent monthly magazine dealing with a wide range of topics. It is available from large newsagents and by subscription from:
British Wildlife Publishing
Lower Barn, Rooks Farm
Rotherwick, Hook,
Hampshire RG27 9BG
Tel: 01256 760663
www.britishwildlife.com

Permaculture
Published quarterly, each issue gives you practical articles and permaculture tips from readers. It is available by subscription from:
Permanent Publications
Freepost (SCE8120)
Petersfield GU32 1HR
Tel: 01730 823311
www.permaculture.co.uk

INDEX